Harrison Burton

The Old-Fashioned Fairy Book

Harrison Burton

The Old-Fashioned Fairy Book

ISBN/EAN: 9783743307582

Manufactured in Europe, USA, Canada, Australia, Japa

Cover: Foto ©ninafisch / pixelio.de

Manufactured and distributed by brebook publishing software (www.brebook.com)

Harrison Burton

The Old-Fashioned Fairy Book

THE PRINCESS EGLANTINE.

CONTENTS.

	PAGE
INTRODUCTION, ...	xiii
THE PRINCESS EGLANTINE, ...	1
DAME MARTHA'S STEP-DAUGHTER; OR, THE GRANDMOTHER OF THE GNOMES, ...	19
THE ADVENTURES OF HA'PENNY; OR, THE DWARF, THE WITCH, AND THE MAGIC SLIPPERS, . . .	47
SYBILLA, MYRTILLO, AND FURIOSO, . . .	69
ANNETTE; OR, THE MAGIC COFFEE-MILL, . .	81
JULIET; OR, THE LITTLE WHITE MOUSE, . .	89
THE FAIRIES AND THE FIDDLER, . . .	107
ETHELINDA; OR, THE ICE KING'S BRIDE, . .	130
DEEP-SEA VIOLETS, ...	149
THE WILD WOODSMAN, ...	178
THE FROZEN HEARTH-FAIRY, ...	185

CONTENTS.

	PAGE
Rosy's Stay-at-Home Parties,	189
Blondina; or, The Turkey-Queen,	211
Timid Agnes,	237
The Ogress and the Cook,	244
Miss Peggy and the Frog,	268
The Leperhaun: A Legend of the Emerald Isle,	276

ROMANCES OF THE MIDDLE AGES.

The Trials of Sir Isumbras,	282
Bisclaveret,	291
Roswal and Lilian,	297
Eliduc and Guilliadun,	308
The Falcon-King,	317
Sir Eglamour and Crystabell,	329

FAIRY DAYS.

Beside the old hall-fire—upon my nurse's knee,
Of happy fairy-days—what tales were told to me!
I thought the world was once—all peopled with princésses,
And my heart would beat to hear—their loves and their distresses;
And many a quiet night—in slumber sweet and deep,
The pretty fairy people—would visit me in sleep.

I saw them in my dreams—come flying east and west,
With wondrous fairy gifts—the new-born babe they bless'd;
One has brought a jewel—and one a crown of gold,
And one has brought a curse—but she is wrinkled and old.
The gentle queen turns pale—to hear those words of sin,
But the king he only laughs—and bids the dance begin.

FAIRY DAYS.

The babe has grown to be—the fairest of the land,
And rides the forest green—a hawk upon her hand,
An ambling palfrey white—a golden robe and crown ;
I've seen her in my dreams—riding up and down :
And heard the ogre laugh—as she fell into his snare,
At the little tender creature—who wept and tore her hair !

But ever when it seemed—her need was at the sorest,
A prince—in shining mail—comes prancing through the forest,
A waving ostrich-plume—a buckler burnished bright ;
I've seen him in my dreams—good sooth ! a gallant knight.
His lips are coral red—beneath a dark moustache ;
See how he waves his hand—and how his blue eyes flash !

" Come forth, thou Paynim knight !"—he shouts in accents clear.
The giant and the maid—both tremble his voice to hear.
Saint Mary guard him well !— He draws his falchion keen,
The giant and the knight—are fighting on the green ;
I see them in my dreams—his blade gives stroke on stroke,
The giant pants and reels—and tumbles like an oak !

With what a blushing grace—he falls upon his knee
And takes the lady's hand—and whispers, "You are free!"
Ah! happy childish tales—of knight and faërie!
I waken from my dreams—but there's ne'er a knight for me;
I waken from my dreams—and wish that I could be
A child by the old hall-fire—upon my nurse's knee!

W. M. THACKERAY.

The Faithful Comrades.

Old-Fashioned Fairies.

INTRODUCTION.

To my Young Readers.

Children Dear:

NOT long ago two little boys, who shall be nameless here, came to their mother's side at that pleasant hour of the twenty-four called by the English "blind-man's holiday," and by the French, "between dog and wolf." The lamps had not been lighted, and the room was full of shadows; but a strip of western sky, seen through the bay window, hung like a pink veil behind which a few pale stars were beginning to show above the dark line of hills. All that bright summer's day long, four little busy feet had been in motion. Directly after breakfast they had raced down the meadow-path, pursued by Colin Clout, their faithful Scotch collie, between grass and daisies so tall that little could be seen of the dog and his younger master, beyond a brown back and white-tipped tail curveting around a scarlet fez that bobbed up and down like a buoy upon the water. Soon the three companions had reappeared for a moment under a low arch of fringy boughs at the entrance to the grove, and then had descended a bank to the edge of a babbling brook, where, on the grassy margin, the children played every day for hours, inventing a hundred devices of boats and dams and waterfalls, whilst Colin lay at ease among the ferns, and from time to time emitted a bark of pure good fellowship. For them this shallow streamlet has a charm hardly to be resisted, even for a summons to drive "over the hills and far away" through the lovely country-side, or to assist in the delights of the season when their pretty meadow grasses are laid low, tossed into fragrant piles, and carted away by merry haying-folk—though sometimes these water-elves pause to forage the neighboring woods for "hocky" sticks and sling-shot crotches, to "shin up" the tall forest trees, or pluck wild strawberries from the sunny slopes beyond their favorite haunt.

On the especial evening of which I write, the faithful comrades had returned, tired, and scratched by the briers of this work-a-day world, from a tramp of some miles in search of live bait for a fishing excursion projected with their father at Lily Pond upon the morrow. The doomed little fishes had been put into a bath-tub full of water, where they were expected to suppose themselves still in their native pool. The boys had been washed and fed—an astonishing supper, even for those cormorants!—and now had elected to seek rest and refreshment at the maternal knee. Colin, observing that everybody else was satisfactorily adjusted in affectionate attitudes, had retired under the fringe of a table-cover close at hand, and lay where only his loving eyes and open mouth could be seen, breathing in short quick pants, or, as the boys called it, "ha-ha-ha-ing at the company."

"And now, mamma, until your tea is ready, we know what you must do," said the children, in a breath. "Tell us a story—a 'real, truly' fairy tale, about a giant and a dwarf, lots and lots of fairies, a prince and a beautiful princess with hair to her very feet, a champion with a magic sword, a dragon-chariot, a witch dressed in snakeskin—and, if you can, an ogre. Don't punish anybody but the witch and the ogre; and *please* don't have any moral, only let everybody 'live in peace and die in a pot of grease,' at the end of it."

"To be sure, we know most of mamma's stories by heart," said the sage elder of nine. "If she could only make up some new ones that aren't in any of our books! Or else, mamma, tell us something you heard a little bit of, long, long ago, from your nurse, and then make up the rest. But whatever one you tell, we'll be sure to like it anyhow."

The stories told, the mother fell to musing, and the result is the little book here presented to the judgment of children other than her own—a few new fairy tales, on the old, old pattern!

In every country of the habitable globe are found the same myths, variously dressed and styled. Let the ethnologist frame what theory he will upon this subject, my own private belief is that once upon a time a good fairy who loved mankind put on the wings of a stormy petrel and flew over many lands, carrying in her hand a sieve full of tiny seeds, and shaking it upon those spots where there appeared to be most children. The seeds, falling to earth after this fashion, sprang up and bore many-colored fairy tales, to rejoice all hearts for evermore. Since then, the fables you and I love have been told from father to son among nations living remote from each other and isolated. The Hindoo toiling under the tropic sun, and the Lapp in his smoky hut banked in snow; the English cottar resting in his ivy-covered porch, and the Russian peasant stretched at length upon the stove which forms his bed; the Persian stroking his gray beard beneath the archways of Ispahan, and the Norwegian carving bits of wood under his rafters of illuminated pine—all know and repeat versions of our favorite tales. In France, in Spain, in Germany—mother of myths—in Italy, where they drop red from the wine-press of Boccaccio—are these stories to be heard. The North American Indian weaves them with his beads and wampum; our southern negro croons them over the corn-cake baking in the spider upon his cabin hearth; the poetical Chinese envelops them in the language of flowers; and the distant dweller by the Amazon embalms them in his legendary lore. So much for the fairy with the sieve!

But great as is the enjoyment had in perusing the fairy tales of different nations, to the child of Anglo-Saxon descent can come no such pleasure so deep as that to be derived from the old romances of our mother country. To me this delight was first revealed by a little fat book that used to be found in our nurseries—the one containing Cinderella, immortal maid—unprincipled Puss in Boots—and Jack, the splendid champion!

Of late years, fairy tales seem to have suffered from their increase of dignity at the hands of grave scholars, who have so dressed them in fine language, and hedged them with innumerable notes and references, that the child shuns the fruit for fear of thorns about it. For my own part, I prefer the older specimens of ancient fairy literature known as chap-books. These were odd little yellow pamphlets, sprinkled with abundant capital letters throughout the text, and "Illustrated with many diverting cutts!" They were carried around the country-side in

INTRODUCTION.

England by peddlers, who sold them (with such other catch-penny wares as ribbons, lace, and trinkets) indifferently at castle gate or cottage lattice; and if you wish to see the sort of fairies your great-grandmothers believed in, look at the three pictures that accompany this preface, copied from a famous chap-book.

There, quaintly depicted, first, appeared Jack in a funny full-bottomed coat, diligently climbing a bean-stalk, where the ogre's castle was perched atop like a bird's nest; lucky Ali-Baba, too; Bluebeard—mighty and pitiless—with Fatima and sister Anne, their back hair down, pleading to him on dislocated knees, their brothers, with drawn swords, galloping to the rescue; and the husband in The Three Wishes, standing agape before his fireside, while his wife danced a jig of rage in her efforts to rid her nose of a pudding little smaller than a feather-bed! There,

INTRODUCTION. xix

also, was displayed that pushing suitor, the Yellow Dwarf, who insisted on attaching to his lady-love's finger a ring made of a single red hair, so fastened that she could not get it off. There was the Desert Fairy, guarded by two lions which the wandering queen endeavored to appease with "a cake made of millet, sugar-candy, and crocodile's eggs." (How we children yearned to taste that cake!) And there were the fascinating White Cat, seated side by side with her enamored prince in a fine calash of blue embossed with gold, the Sleeping Beauty, the Babes in the Wood—hapless cherubs—the Girl who dropped pearls and diamonds when she spoke, dear Graciosa and ready Percinet, gallant Riquet-with-the-Tuft, and Goody Two Shoes—the latter a little of a prig, I fear—clever Hop o' my Thumb, Beauty and the Beast, Little Red Riding-hood—the long procession of charmers to whom even now my heart bows in salutation as I write their familiar names!

Chap-books of ancient date have been recently reproduced in England; from one of them, I have taken the substance of a story I never chanced to see elsewhere, and under the title of "Juliet; or, the Little White Mouse" have given it to you in language of my own.

After the chap-books came other cheap fairy publications, notably those of Mr. Newberry, a good old gentleman who, in the last century, sent out numberless sixpenny booklets, many of them reaching America to give pleasure to the infants of the colonies. Washington Irving goes so far as to say that if George Washington had not read Newberry's publications in his youth, especially "Whittington and his Cat," he would not have been the first and greatest President of the United States! The grave Benjamin Franklin, while a printer in Philadelphia, emulated Newberry in publishing nursery tales, and no doubt devoured them himself with relish.

Many a pen of the great in history or literature has found a theme in these favorites of ours. Of Cinderella, the famous Canning, premier of England, wrote in glowing rhyme:

> "Six bobtailed mice transport her to the ball,
> And liveried lizards wait upon her call."

And Thackeray has thrown around fairy lore the rays of his noble genius, not only in the lines already here quoted, but in a Christmas story so enchanting that, if you are unfortunate enough not already to have made acquaintance with Valoroso and Gruffanuff, Bulbo and Angelica, I urge you to try at once the magician's art and coax "The Rose and the Ring" out of the pocket of your nearest relative. By the giant Thackeray, when entangled in the meshes of Fairydom, one is reminded of Gulliver under bonds to the Lilliputians, yet wearing his bonds so easily!

INTRODUCTION.

And now, I leave my new-old Fairy Book to you, my little critics. I am sure you will accord a generous welcome to the pictures. What would our benighted great-grandmothers have said to Miss Emmet's charming illustrations?

C. C. H.

THE PRINCESS EGLANTINE.

 CERTAIN queen had twin children, a boy and a girl, both as beautiful as the dawn of a summer morning. As the mother was one day hanging over the double cradle, shaped like two silver lilies growing on one stem, an old aunt of hers, who knew a good deal about magic, arrived from the country to see the babies and to spend the day.

The old lady took the Princess Eglantine in her arms, and kissed her, and joggled her, and clucked at her, after the fashion of all good aunties.

"That's a girl to be proud of, my dear!" she said,

handing the baby back to her mamma. "And she looks as good as she is pretty, too."

"They are both *wonderful* children, nurse says," replied the young queen, modestly. "And the doctor thinks them the *finest pair* he has ever seen. Only the boy is *a little* high-tempered. He kicks and snaps at his attendants the whole time he is awake; so take care, aunty dear, and don't disturb him for the world. We always let him sleep as long as he will."

"Hoity-toity!" cried aunty, "as if I came out of the woods to be frightened by an owl. *I* know how to manage *all* children!" and the boy opening his eyes at that moment, she lifted him from his crib, and laid him on her lap.

Sad to say, he behaved like an infant tiger. Never was there seen such a tempestuous baby. He wriggled, and howled, and fought, and plunged, until the poor mother and nurses turned red with mortification. But the old aunty held on to him bravely, and examined him from top to toe. Nothing could she find, till she came to the sole of the right foot, and there was a tiny red mark like a burning torch. As soon as aunty saw this she sighed, and whispered a word in the baby's ear, when he became as quiet as any lamb.

Aunty sent away the nurses, and told the poor queen there was no doubt about it; her boy was bewitched, and when he grew up he would try to devour his sister. The only thing was to keep them apart, and this the queen told her husband; and he sent for a wise man, who confirmed what aunty had said. The wise man added that all would go well so long as the princess was kept apart from her brother, and as the brother was the heir of the kingdom, there was nothing left but to banish the unfortunate princess. The king built for his daughter, in the remotest corner of his kingdom, an ivory tower. Around the tower was a crystal moat full of gold and silver fish. Around the moat were lovely flower-beds, and around the flower-beds was a thick and thorny hedge. In this tower there was a room lined with tufted blue satin, like the inside of a bonbon box, and all the furniture was made of fine carved ivory. Here the princess was shut up for life, under the care of an old dame, Madame Véloutine by name, who once had kept a boarding-school for duchesses, and was very respectable indeed. Poor Eglantine was gradually forgotten at court, and her cannibal brother grew up without knowing he had ever had a sister.

Like all other captive princesses, past, present, and to come, Eglantine was beautiful and accomplished. She could speak in every language, work in silk and crewels, paint china plaques, make mince-pies, sing like a nightingale, and play anything on the piano at sight with her eyes shut! Her skin was milk-white, with a rosy flush on the cheeks, while her glorious golden hair never came out of crimp, but rippled from the roots to her very feet.

One day a prince, cantering by upon his palfrey, looked up at the tower window, and there saw this lovely creature, surrounded by a flock of pretty white doves. Prince Charming gazed and gazed, and the longer he stood there, the more enraptured he became. When he heard from the country people that no one knew who or what was this mysterious beauty, excepting that once a year, by night, a grand gentleman and lady visited her, and looked at her while asleep, the ardent young prince made a vow to solve the secret without delay. He engaged his old tutor to make love to Eglantine's governess, and this plan succeeded so well that the tutor was, ere long, invited to take a cup of tea at five o'clock, in the ground-floor apartment of the tower where Madame Véloutine kept house. Madame Véloutine was very much fluttered by the attentions of the tutor, a gloomy-looking individual with savage dark mustache and deep-sunken eyes. The poor old thing, who had been reading novels without any intermission for eighteen years, was very sentimental, and the idea of a suitor coming to woo at some period of her existence was never wholly absent from her thoughts. She dressed herself in one of the Princess Eglantine's white robes, put a blue sash around her waist, and covering her little red nose with rice powder, sat in a darkened corner with a guitar upon her knees. The tutor flattered her, and soon she grew confidential and told him the story of her charge. When the tutor took his leave, Madame Véloutine sighed deeply, and pitied the poor man who had fallen a victim to her charms. She did not see the fat purse of gold the prince bestowed on him, upon learning the true state of the case about the enchanting captive!

Prince Charming rode, day and night, till he reached the king's palace. "Give me your daughter for my wife," he said. The king turned pale at hearing that the secret was betrayed. "For pity's sake speak lower, young man," said the anxious father. "Only suppose her brother should hear of it." With that he told the whole story to Prince Charming, who forthwith rode to ask a wise man what he should do to set the princess free, with safety to herself.

"Ride as far as you will, and as fast as you will with her, you may not escape the curse," said the wise man.

The prince went off heavy-hearted, and visited a witch he knew. She was knitting a stocking, which ravelled every night as fast as it grew by day.

"I have been knitting this stocking for fifty years," said the witch, taking a pinch of snuff out of the souptureenful that she always kept beside her. "I could as soon make it whole in one night as keep away the curse from her."

The prince groaned as he rode away. Across his path was a green bough, half covered by a huge cobweb. In this a tiny being, no bigger than a fly, was entangled, and was making desperate struggles to be free. Travelling toward it, with tremendous strides, came an enormous red spider, with white spots and great protruding eyes. The prince, not without a shudder, for, like most of us, he hated the nasty things, killed the spider with a blow, and set free the pretty captive, who proved to be a fairy. She tidied her iridescent frock, and thanked him very nicely.

"You have saved my life, dear prince," she said. "Pray let me do something in return for it."

"Perhaps you can help me," said the prince, eagerly. "If you can't, never mind," he added, politely, when he had finished telling her the sad story of his doomed princess. "I don't expect much of a person of your size, you know; but really it's the greatest *relief* to talk about the dear darling!"

"A person of my size!" said the little lady, with a shrill sniff. "I'd have you to know, prince, that I'm the fairy Buz-fuz, the discoverer of the celebrated invisibility powder. It is *never* known to fail, is made from a fern-seed that *I* alone can pluck, and is *not* for sale at *any* druggist's! As to lifting the spell from that poor young creature, the princess, I can't undertake to do it, on any terms; but with the aid of my powder, one pinch of which sprinkled on an object will make it disappear from sight in a moment, I believe you can manage to keep clear of the cannibal brother."

The prince thanked the fairy, took the powder, and galloped off, light-hearted, to his Eglantine. She, poor thing, had thought of nothing but the prince and his beauty, and his kind glances and smiles, since he left her. She wearied of the society of poor old Véloutine, and sighed for change. Véloutine was in despair. To comfort the princess she promised to allow her a single meeting with the prince, should he ever come that way again. "That I am sure he will!" said the princess. "If you had only seen his eyes when he looked at me! They were so kind, so true! Oh! Véloutine! he *will* come back!"

So Eglantine settled down to her embroidery. This was a gown of white damask with large white satin flowers outlined with real pearls. She had been at work on it for several years, and a few stitches more would finish it. She now wrought busily, until the last stitch was set, and then, with trembling fingers, put it on. Around her neck and waist she wrapped great chains of pearls, and left her long hair rippling to her knees. When her toilet was complete she went to the window. It was the sunset of a summer's day. Around her tower grew vines heavy with deep-red roses; the shining surface of the moat beneath was streaked with color from the western clouds. Along the path beyond the hedge rode a horseman gayly clad in green and gold, who, smiling, doffed a cap with a single long white plume, and bowed to his saddle-bow. Behind him came a splendid cavalcade of courtiers and knights on horseback, surrounding a golden coach in which sat the father and mother of Eglantine, who had given consent to her marriage with the prince. The poor king and queen were dreadfully frightened at the rashness of this proceeding. They had sent the cannibal brother off on a hunting excursion in a distant part of the country, and had come in fear and trembling, bringing with them the most trustworthy of their people. They could not resist Prince Charming, who, in addition to his other attractions, had just lost his father, the old king, and was now the sole owner and ruler of a neighboring kingdom, and just the match for their lovely daughter. He had sworn to them that their child should be kept so securely guarded that her brother could never reach her.

Eglantine came down from her bower, to be introduced to her father, mother, and lover all at once. The marriage took place without delay, and the new king started with his bride for the sea-shore, where they were to embark for his home.

They set sail in a ship of which the sides were plated with beaten gold. The sails were of pink satin, and the ropes golden threads plaited together. The young king and queen sat upon cushions of velvet on the deck, and talked of their happy future, when suddenly the sky was darkened as by a cloud, and, riding upon a vulture, the cannibal brother came after them. He had been hunting, and a wandering breeze carried to him the story of his sister's escape. Although he had never before heard he possessed a sister, the first whisper of such a thing was sufficient to rouse in him the dreadful cannibal instinct to drink her blood. From where the king and queen sat they could distinctly hear him smacking his lips with joy at the prospect of his horrible meal. Queen Eglantine, fearing she knew not what, shuddered from head to foot, and closing her eyes cast herself upon the king's breast for protection.

The king, bidding her be calm, sprinkled the deck of the ship with one of the fairy's powders, which he carried in a little crystal box. At the moment the huge foul bird of prey hovered above them and gave a fierce swoop downward, the ship and all its contents vanished utterly from sight, while the vulture with his rider plunged into the sea.

The cannibal prince was a good swimmer, and although his vulture was immediately drowned, managed to keep up, until he found a dolphin and got astride its back.

"Now, carry me in pursuit of yonder ship, and mind you swim fast and well," he exclaimed.

"Master, I obey," said the dolphin, who recognized in him a magician. "But, look for yourself—blue sky above, blue water below, and not a sail upon the sea."

The prince looked, and in truth there was no ship to be seen; so, ordering the dolphin to convey him to the nearest landing-place, he soon reached the shores of a beautiful country, where flags were flying, and all the inhabitants were dressed in holiday clothes. Over the wharf was an arch of most lovely flowers, and five hundred little girls were strewing the roads with orange blossoms.

"What is taking place?" asked the cannibal brother of the people around the wharf.

"Where have *you* been, pray?" said they scornfully, "not to know that our king brings home his bride to-day!"

Then the ship came in sight and the rejoicings began. The cannibal brother had no sooner laid eyes upon his sister than a new longing to drink her blood came over him; and he set about plotting how he could get hold of her, no easy matter, since the palace was guarded night and day by twenty white bull-dogs of the fiercest sort, besides the usual soldiers and attendants. So he took service with a butcher near the town, and made a bag full of little meat-balls, each one containing a drop of deadly poison. One day his master sent him to the palace to carry Queen Eglantine's sweetbreads and mutton-chops. "Now," thought the brother, "I shall get inside;" but he was mistaken, for the sweetbreads and mutton-chops were taken from him at the gate, and passed on through twenty different hands till they reached the cook. As no outsider whatever was allowed to penetrate the inner palace walls, behind which the new queen lived surrounded by every luxury, the cannibal brother had to wait many days for an opportunity to get a sight of her. Meantime his appetite was gaining terribly, and he went to the blacksmith and had all his teeth framed in iron, the better to enjoy his horrid meal.

At last King Charming was summoned to meet a neighboring monarch about a right of way for his armies across a certain peninsula; and, with many injunctions to the queen not to admit any stranger during his absence, he reluctantly set out. No sooner was he out of sight than the pretended butcher's boy hastened to assume his own princely clothing, and, ringing boldly at the castle gate, told the servants to announce to the queen that her brother had arrived, bearing messages from her father and mother. He sent in a golden locket containing likenesses of both the king and queen, his parents, which convinced Queen Eglantine that his tale was true. So, joyfully, she ran forth to meet him, and would have cast herself upon his neck, but that the trained bull-dogs rushed between, growling most horribly.

"Come here, pretty fellow, nice fellow," said the cannibal brother, coaxingly; but the dogs only opened their jaws wider than before and growled defiance.

"Give them these little dainties, sister," said the wily prince, producing his poisoned meat-balls. "They are some that I always carry for my own pets."

The innocent queen called the dogs one after another to her side, and fed them with the fatal balls, which they ate, licking her white hand gratefully. At once, as the poison began to work, they all lay down in a row, and became as quiet as they had been before ferocious. The queen led her brother into an inner room, and bade him sit upon her silken couch. The prince laughed to himself, for now, thought he, the hour has come for my coveted meal. But he was seized with the notion to go into another room in order to file his teeth, which were becoming rather dull.

"Will you not play for me upon the piano, sister?" he asked lovingly.

The amiable queen, who never waited to be asked twice, sat down to play, while her brother hid within a closet and began to file his teeth. Up jumped the queen's cat, in great excitement, and sat on her mistress' lap.

"Mistress dear," said the affectionate creature, "fly, fly, as fast as your feet will carry you. Your brother is at this moment getting ready to make a meal of you, and as he is a magician no one in the castle is strong enough to defend you from him. In the stable you will find the king's gray steed. Jump upon his back, and be off, while I play the piano in your stead."

The terrified queen took to her royal heels, weeping as she stumbled over the dead bodies of her faithful dogs, and the clever cat sat playing beautifully so many runs and trills that the prince, admiring his sister's brilliant execution, made no haste to leave his task until it was finished to his entire satisfaction.

And now, mounted upon the good gray steed, away flew Queen Eglantine in search of her beloved spouse. Pretty soon she heard footsteps, and there, swifter than any horse, swifter than wind, on flew the cannibal brother after her.

"What shall I do, dear steed?" said the alarmed queen.

"Drop your cloak into the road," said the gray horse, who was the cat's own cousin.

The queen obeyed, and the cloak became a broad lake, across which the cannibal brother took a long time to swim. The gray horse got a good start, but presently the prince came nearly up with him.

"What shall I do now, dear steed?" said the queen, almost ready to fall fainting from his back.

"Drop the veil from your head," said the horse.

This was done, and the veil became a thick fog, causing the cannibal brother to lose his way and stumble dreadfully. But he got out of it at last, and came nearly up with them.

"What shall I do next, dear steed?" said the queen, trembling in every limb.

"Take your scissors and cut a long lock from your hair, and throw that behind you."

The queen lifted the scissors that hung at her girdle, and in a moment, snip! they went into her beautiful golden hair. The hair became a jungle of tall reeds, and through it the cannibal brother had work indeed to travel. While he was puffing and blowing and struggling in the reeds, oh, joy! the queen saw her king riding swiftly to meet her.

Just as the cannibal brother, by a desperate effort of magic strength had freed himself from the jungle, and emerged in swift pursuit, he had the mortification of seeing the queen rush into her husband's arms. His dreadful hunger was now increased until it drove him to desperation. With a roar of baffled rage he darted toward the royal couple, swearing that both of them should be his victims; and this no doubt would have been the case—since the monster was endowed with the strength of fifty men—but that the king, bidding his queen have no fear, quickly sprinkled them both, and their steeds, with a pinch of the fairy fern-seed. Immediately they disappeared from sight, and the cannibal brother, coming with full force upon the spot where they had been, beheld only empty space.

This disappointment, combined with his now really appalling appetite, made the miserable wretch fall in a fit upon the ground.

The king would have killed him where he lay, but the queen pleaded for her brother's life, so the attendants bore him, insensible, back to the palace. There, the queen's clever cat advised that he should be left to her to deal with. She shut herself up with the patient in a tower bedroom, and during sixty days and nights not a morsel of food passed the sufferer's lips, except the cat's magic castor-oil—a cupful every ten minutes— each tasting more nauseous than the one before! In the morning he was lifted from bed, and put into an ice-cold bath, and then whipped soundly until his circulation was restored. At the end of the second month the cat stopped his bath, whipping, and medicines, offering him instead a handful of parched peas and a dry crust. This diet seemed to him so delicious that never again could he be tempted to vary it. Until he reached a green and virtuous old age this prince was never known to look upon so much as a rare beefsteak without shuddering! His father, mother, sister, and brother-in-law united their tears of joy at this happy reform, and who should the clever cat turn out to be, but aunty, who had taken this means of watching over her favorite Eglantine ! The gray steed was aunty's first cousin upon the mother's side ; but when peace was restored he preferred to go back to his own country to live, although the grateful King Charming offered him every inducement to remain, in the way of marble stalls and silver mangers, rose-water to quench his thirst, and golden oats to eat. Aunty, too, retired to her own distant castle, and the reformed cannibal lived quiet and happy until the time came to reign in his good father's stead.

As for Eglantine and King Charming, they never again found use for the fern-seed powder. Even the faults of one were invisible to the other.

Nothing occurred to disturb the serenity of their entire reign but a suit for breach-of-promise of marriage, brought against the king's former tutor by the queen's former governess, Madame Véloutine ; and this was settled speedily by the tutor announcing that, rather than make any fuss about the matter, he would marry the old lady and be done with it, although he really could not imagine what there had been in his past conduct to put such an idea into her venerable head. So at last Véloutine got a husband, and nobody could be surprised at anything after that.

DAME MARTHA'S STEP-DAUGHTER;

OR,

THE GRANDMOTHER OF THE GNOMES.

DAME MARTHA lived at the foot of a high mountain. Her cottage was large enough to give shelter only to herself and two young girls, one of them her own child and the other the child of Dame Martha's late husband, who, about six months before this story opens, slipped down a fissure in the rocks and had nevermore been seen. Dame Martha did not bear a very good character in the neighborhood, as she was known to be violent in temper and dishonest in her dealings. While her husband lived, she had quarrelled with him from morning till night, and after he disappeared, people used to hint that Dame Martha knew better than any one else how the poor man came to his sudden death. But nothing was ever proved upon her, and as the dame's cottage stood in a desolate valley, overshadowed by a frowning cliff on which grew a single lightning-blasted pine-tree, children shunned the lonely spot, and few grown people found anything to attract them in that direction. Margaret, the dame's own daughter, was a handsome haughty lass of about nineteen, so spoiled and self-willed that she bid fair to rival her mother in temper, in the course of time. Hilda, the step-daughter, was a fair and gentle little creature, sixteen years of age, who bore with patient cheerfulness all the unhappiness of her lot. Sometimes, for days together, she would be left alone in the house, while Dame Martha and Margaret dressed themselves up in all their finery, and went off to fairs and merrymakings in the neighboring town. Melancholy were the hours spent in a solitude unbroken save by the rush of the waterfall leaping from cliff to cliff, or the hootings of owls after nightfall, and the unceasing wail of the wind through the forest. But Hilda was at least spared the sound of Margaret's taunting voice and laugh, and the cruel scolding tongue of her step-mother. These two wicked women were heartily tired of Hilda, and cast about in their minds how they could get rid of her, and take possession of a little bag of gold pieces coming to her from her father. Then, thought they, the old house could be shut up and left to the rats and bats, while they might set out on their travels and enjoy life.

One day, when Hilda was bleaching the linen on a patch of grass near the brook, her step-mother called out, "Hilda, the red cow has strayed away, and I hear her bell over by the old stone quarry. Be quick, and you may head her off."

Hilda secured her linen, and with nimble steps, ran up the steep mountain side. She did not fancy the idea of going by the old stone quarry, for there it had been, six months before, that her dear father was last seen in life. Near that spot his hat and shepherd-staff had been found. But Hilda was accustomed to obey without remonstrance, and away she ran, climbing as lightly as a mountain goat. She too, could hear the tinkle of the little bell far up among the bushes, and guided by the sound, she drew near the dreaded scene of her greatest sorrow. A thick screen of fir bushes lay between her and the red cow's place of refuge. Interwoven with evergreens, grew masses of alpine-rose, whose tough branches became entangled in Hilda's feet, and hid the path from sight. At last, she found herself in a dense thicket, not knowing how to emerge. As she paused for a moment to look about her, the red cow's bell tinkled again—a strange uncertain tinkle this—immediately behind the bushes at her left.

"There you are, good-for-nothing!" cried Hilda, struggling bravely forward through the undergrowth in the direction indicated by the bell. She heard a low mocking laugh. Surely that laugh could come only from her step sister! "Margaret!" she called. No answer, and poor Hilda, uttering a wild shriek for help, plunged headlong down a hidden opening in the ground, into a fathomless abyss, where no foot of man might follow her.

Wicked Margaret stood on the brink of this treacherous pit-fall, known only to her mother and herself, and laughed, holding in her hand the little red cow's bell, with which she had lured Hilda to her doom.

"Rest there!" the wretched girl said, kneeling down to peer into the darkness of the rocky pit. "At any rate, you have found a burial-place for your bones, alongside of your father, who was never heard to groan after my mother and I pushed him over the brink here, last autumn! And now, I will go home, and tell the old woman that we are rid of all our burdens. Ha! ha! Won't we spend the father's gold, and revel! This very night must we steal away, and seek our fortune in a distant country."

Hilda fell, unharmed, upon a hillock of soft green moss, so far, so far beneath the ledge whence Margaret had pushed her, that the opening above looked no bigger than a star. The poor girl was overcome by her terrible fate, and for a long time she lay weeping as if her heart would break. Then, looking about her, she saw the opening to a cavern in the rocks, resembling an arch of crystal, so bravely did it glitter.

Around the hillock where she lay was a small court-yard with turf as smooth as velvet, and upon the rocky walls encircling it were trained vines of roses, myrtle and jasmine, covered with lovely blossoms. Hilda, who knew best the alp-rose and the corn-flower, the hardy violet and the rock-seeking columbine, had never seen such rare and radiant flowers as these, and their rich perfume intoxicated her with delight. Stealing down the side of the cliff, trickled a sparkling rivulet, its stream caught in a basin of gleaming pearl.

Hilda, enchanted by the lovely scene, forgot her grief, and felt a longing desire to follow the path of many-colored pebbles leading beneath the crystal arch. Without a token of fear, she tripped along this pretty path winding through a gallery supported by pillars of frosted silver. Here and there glowed a lamp of pink, blue or crimson, fashioned like a flower. Strains of sweet music were heard in the distance, and at last Hilda reached a gate of golden trellis-work, beside which slept a tiny old man, whose beard and hair fell over his red mantle to the very ground.

"He is very old, and no doubt needs his rest," said Hilda; "I won't disturb him, poor old man." So she sat down on the ground at his feet, and every time his head nodded to his knees, she would pick up the queer little red cap that fell off of it, and put it on again. After a long, comfortable nap, the old fellow woke up, and saw Hilda sitting at his feet.

"You are a kind maiden," he said, for he was of a race that know everything without waiting to be told —the Gnomes. "Since you have been so good to me, I will let you pass the wicket. Six months ago your father came this way, and if you can but make friends with our mistress, you may be allowed to see him."

"My father! My dear father!" cried Hilda, overjoyed. "Oh! you good, kind gateman, do lead me to where he is."

"Hush! not a sound," said the Gnome, looking about him in alarm. "Everything has ears and tongues too in this place. One warning will I give you. Answer not when spoken to, serve faithfully, break nothing, show no surprise; and when you can capture the bird that bathes daily in the fountain of life, save the drops from off his plumage. Now go on; and farewell, as no one who passes me comes back this way."

Hilda was frightened by the mystery of the warning, but continued on her way, through a long and winding passage in the rocks, dimly lighted here and there by hanging lamps of alabaster. Reaching another little wicket-gate of golden trellis-work, she summoned all her courage and rang the bell. Out came a hideous crone, whose ears, grown to an enormous size, hung down upon her neck, and who, without asking her business, opened the gate.

"If ears grow like this," thought Hilda, "I had, indeed, better hold my tongue and say nothing to give offence." So, pretending to be dumb, she curtsied to the crone, and made signs that she wanted food and drink. The old woman led Hilda along the path of a neglected garden, to a house built of gray lichen from the bark of trees, and thatched with hoary moss. The

windows were barred, and in the open doorway sat a cross old dame, at her knitting. She had a hump, ears larger than those of the lodge-keeper, and claws hooked like an eagle's.

"What! another of those foolish mortals fallen down our pit!" she cried, angrily; "I have half a mind to kill her on the spot." But Hilda looked so meek and imploring, standing there and saying not a word, that the Grandmother of the Gnomes relented. "Well, well," she grunted, "although she is decidedly overgrown, and has ridiculously small ears, I suppose I may as well try her for a nurse-maid. If she proves unfaithful, there will be plenty to tell of it, and she will soon go the way of all the rest."

Hilda was pleased at the idea of being a nurse-maid, for she always got on well with children. She followed the G. G. (really, if you will excuse me, it will save a great deal of trouble sometimes to abbreviate the old lady's title) inside the queer little house, and there was a room full of owls, bats, toads, mice, and spiders, who came flocking around the new-comer, with every expression of delight.

"Oh! you pretty darlings!" cried the old woman, kissing them rapturously, "here is a new nurse for you; and mind you keep her busy."

When Hilda found that she was expected to bathe, and clean, and walk out with, and sleep with these loathsome creatures, she felt that she had rather die. But fear of the terrible G. G. kept her silent, and setting about her task, she soon had them ready for an airing in the garden. Here she beheld many strange sights, but nothing more curious than to see all the bushes and plants and trees bearing large ears, which, as she drew near, became erect and fixed in an attitude of attention. Remembering the caution of the friendly gnome to express no surprise, Hilda drove her little flock before her along the garden path, then returning to the house, fed them and put them to bed in the most orderly fashion. For reward, she found, on a bench outside the door, a nice bowl of milk with fine white bread and butter, and after devouring it eagerly, she fell asleep. When she awoke next day, Hilda found herself in another garden. This one was most beautiful. All the rose-bushes had gold or silver leaves, and flowers made of jewels. She longed to twitch off one of the shining leaves, but dared not, contenting herself with watering their roots and neatly clearing up the paths, as the Gnome Grandmother had directed her. For reward, she had a bowl of delicious hot soup, and a cup

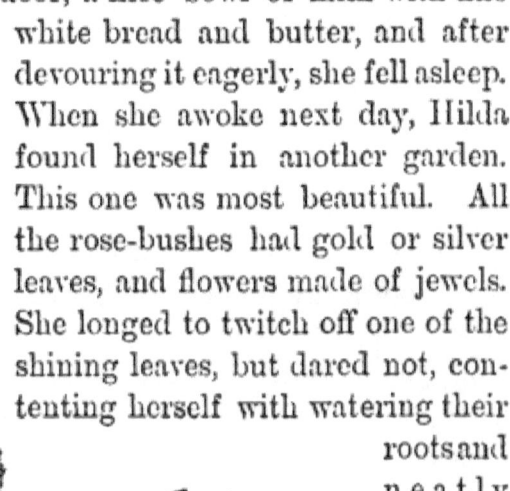

of amber jelly, and falling asleep, she awakened next day in still another garden. Here sported birds of radiant hue and plumage, singing delightfully, as they flitted about the brim of a great marble fountain on a grassy lawn, surrounded by blooming flowers.

"Here, children, I bring you a new nurse-maid," said the Gnome Grandmother, presenting her to the birds; and immediately, the lovely creatures surrounded Hilda, perching on her arms, her head, her shoulders, and caressing her with evident pleasure.

"Now that you have successfully met my three tests—the first, of your fidelity, by doing your duty toward the creatures you abhorred; secondly, by passing through my jewel-garden without plucking a flower or leaf; thirdly, by showing no surprise at the wonders you have seen—you have proved yourself worthy to be the keeper of my birds," said the old woman. "It is well for you that the ears have heard no grumbling. And mind you go on as you've begun."

Hilda thanked her with beaming glances, but would not venture to speak, although she longed to ask news of her dear father. "To those who wait, all things come in time," she remembered her father used to say, and determined not to break silence yet a while. The

Grandmother of the Gnomes disappeared, and Hilda set herself to the task of caring for her new and lovely pets. Around the garden were bowers of sweet-smelling honeysuckle, and in each of these hung a silver cage. Hilda's duty was to cover the bottoms of the cages with sand of broken diamonds, to gather fresh sprays of flowers to stick between their bars, and to fill the jewelled drinking-troughs with dew from the cups of flowers. Day after day passed in attendance upon the birds, who all became devoted to her, in return. Each morning the Grandmother of the Gnomes came into the garden, and sometimes even smiled on Hilda, her grin making her ugliness and deformity seem to increase, if possible. Still Hilda dared not speak the words that were always trembling on her tongue. When night came, the young girl retired to rest in a delightful little house shaped from a bush of growing box, out of which doors and windows had been cut. Within was a bed of moss like velvet, and a coverlet made of the woven wings of the butterfly, with blankets of swansdown. Her meals were served by unseen hands. Punctually at breakfast, dinner, and tea-time, there sprang up in the bower-house a little table shaped like a huge mushroom, covered with dainty food in dishes of gold and silver. New clothes were prepared for her, and laid across the foot of her couch while she slept. Among them were gauzy gowns that seemed to have been cut from the clouds after sunset, cobweb handkerchiefs, shoes made of mole-skin, and necklaces of petrified dew-drops. Hilda might have been quite happy but for the continual thought that her father was imprisoned somewhere near, and her longing to find him and tell him she was there. One night, while she lay thinking, apparently asleep, footsteps came to the side of her bed, and stopped. Somebody held a lamp close to her face, but Hilda pretended to be in a deep slumber, and soon the G. G., for she it was, went away, pattering about the bower, and talking to the old lodge-keeper, who followed her.

"She is sound asleep, so come along. We are already a little late for our round among the prisoners. Foolish creatures! Why hadn't they, too, the sense to restrain themselves as this child did, and they might all have been working in the gardens, to this day. But no! Each one must needs twitch off a leaf here, or a rose there, and stare, and chatter over what they saw, or else go into convulsions over the work given them to do for my pretty toads, and bats, and serpents.

That silly father of hers, for example! He seemed an honest fellow, but what should he do, when he thought no one was looking, but pluck one of my choicest ruby roses to carry back to Hilda. Hum! much likelihood there is that Hilda ever finds out where he is hidden, after a crime like that!"

The Grandmother of the Gnomes seemed to have worked herself up into such an angry state, that Hilda dared not give any sign of waking. So she lay, still as a mouse, till the old couple had laid across her couch the new robe for next day, and trotted off. Then, gliding swiftly from her bed, the girl followed them, down a long green alley of the garden, to a grassy bank she had often noticed. There, putting her hand upon a trap-door, half hidden from sight by a mass of vines, the old crone knocked thrice, saying, "Open to the Grandmother of the Gnomes!"

The door opened, and behind it was a narrow passageway guarded by two dwarfs in red. No one spoke, and the dwarfs, prostrating themselves upon their faces, remained motionless while their sovereign lady passed in. Hilda seized this opportunity to follow, and crept unnoticed to the mouth of a circular vault of gray granite, hung with curtains of black velvet and lighted by swinging lamps of lurid red. In the centre was a long row of white marble tombs, and on each one of these tombs lay a human being apparently asleep, enclosed in a crystal casket. With a thrill of emotion, Hilda recognized in one of these placid sleepers her beloved father. The Grandmother of the Gnomes walked past each bier, sprinkling it with the liquid from a vial in her hand. At once the sleepers aroused and sat up, rolling their eyes and extending their arms to her with a beseeching gesture. The G. G. sternly shook her head, and proceeded to open a little door in each casket, through which the old lodge-keeper gave food and drink to all the prisoners in turn. The poor wretches ate and drank in silence, then turning over on their sides, the crone waved her wand above them, and instantly they fell again into a trance-like sleep.

"Sleep now, till this day week!" said the Grandmother of the Gnomes, solemnly, retiring as she came. Hilda hid in a nook of the wall of rock, and followed her guides out, noiselessly and unnoticed by the prostrate dwarfs in red.

And now her sole thought was how she might get possession of the reviving liquid. Alone and unprotected as she was, at the mercy of her gnome mistress, Hilda knew not where to turn for help. In the extremity of her distress, she thought of what the friendly gnome at the outer gate had said to her. "When you can capture the bird that bathes in the water of life, save the drops from off his plumage." But although Hilda racked her brain for a solution of the mystery, none could she find. All day long her birds came and went among the branches of the beautiful garden, and at night returned to their silver cages in the honeysuckle bowers. The only bath she had ever seen them take, was in the wide marble basin on the grass-plot beneath the fountain. At last, lying down to rest one day upon a bank of lilies, she fell asleep, and in her dreams, heard two of the birds talking on the bough above.

"To-morrow, our friend, the little brown wren returns from his travels to the Spring of Life," said one of them.

"Yes, he has been gone longer than usual, this time," said the other. "What a lucky creature he is to have gained our mistress's favor, and to be allowed to take those baths, which have the power to make him know everything, live forever, and sing more sweetly than the nightingale."

"There is something mysterious about that wren, undoubtedly," sighed the first bird. "Nobody knows whether it is fear or favor that gains so many more privileges for him than for the rest of us. Do you know that if he should ever drop the single golden feather in his tail, he will become like the rest of us again, a slave and captive? And the lucky person who finds it, will be able to see all the hidden treasures of the caves beneath the mountain, pierce his way through solid rock and iron, and even defy the authority of our Sovereign Lady herself!"

Hilda listened, her heart beating high with hope. Next day, indeed, there came a new bird among her charges, a little brown wren, who sat upon the topmost twig of the highest tree in the garden, and dried and smoothed his feathers, singing so exquisitely that all the others gathered around him in delight, while the disconsolate lark and nightingale, canary, mocking-bird and wood-robin, retired to a thicket of green leaves, and wept for jealousy.

Spite of all Hilda's blandishments and wiles, the little brown wren would never come near enough for her to handle him. She could see him, flying amid the upper branches, the single golden feather in his tail shining splendidly, but nothing secured his presence within reach or touch. Even the Grandmother of the Gnomes was powerless to control the wilful creature.

Weeks passed and Hilda was always on guard to follow the Gnome Grandmother and her attendant upon their expeditions to the crypt where the prisoners were kept. By means of the stratagem she had first employed, she never failed to be present when her father was so mysteriously recalled to life, and then dismissed again into the shadowy border-land of death. Although she could not speak to him, or tell him she was near, it was some comfort to see him arise up strong and well. Oh! if the day should come, when she might capture that tantalizing little brown bird! He had become less shy with her of late, and more inclined to perch upon the branch above her head, and, while keeping a safe distance, observe her motions closely. At last, one evening, quite disheartened, Hilda went within her own little bowery house, and sat her down and wept. For the first time since her arrival in the gnome garden, she spoke aloud.

"Oh! I can bear it no longer. My heart will break! My heart will break."

To Hilda's utter astonishment, a voice came from the foliage around her window, in reply.

"Cheer up, dear maiden; the sound of a human voice has broken the spell cast over me, and I now see you as you are. I am he whom you have known as the little brown bird, in reality a mortal prince, bewitched by that wicked old woman, the Grandmother of the Gnomes, who makes everything within her kingdom subservient to her power. She is my deadly enemy, because I once discovered the secret of her fountain of life;

Hilda listens to the little brown bird.

and, when on a journey thither with my followers, I was captured and changed into my present shape, while they, poor creatures, were carried prisoners to her crypt. Should I regain my shape, it can only be done by the help of a being brave and true like yourself."

"But why, why did you not make friends with me at first?" said the joyful Hilda.

"The spell cast upon me forbade my recognizing one of my own kind, unless she or he spoke, and you know how human speech is punished in this place. For three long years I have lived in solitude, compelled by the crone to fly back and forth to fetch her the water of life for her magical incantations; what I receive upon my own plumage, while drawing the water for her, has, however, secured my immortality. As for my golden plume it is the magic blade presented to me at birth, by a wonderful old wiseman, who said that it would point me to the treasures beneath the earth, defy the powers of evil, and pierce its way through solid rock. This sword, the Grandmother of the Gnomes was unable, much as she wished to do so, to deprive me of. The utmost she could accomplish was to transform it into a golden plume. Should I ever be so unfortunate as to drop it, the finder will be my conqueror. See what confidence I have in your goodness of heart, when I thus give my life into your hands."

"Never could I be so base as to betray you, dear prince," said Hilda joyfully.

"Oh! speak on, loveliest of maidens," cried the disguised prince. "Every syllable you utter brings back life and hope to my sad heart. Strange that I should have watched you come and go without knowing what you are. It was the first utterance of your silvery voice in lamentation that awakened my benumbed senses. Now, shall we not work together for our deliverance?"

Gladly did Hilda pour forth all the story of her woes to her newly found confidant. The prince bade her to be of good cheer, for it was his intention to set forth on the morrow upon his monthly journey in search of the water of life.

"A week hence I shall return, and although it would be impossible for me to secrete any of the precious fluid so that our mistress would fail to find it out, yet I will take care to saturate my plumage with the water, so that you can obtain enough to free your father and the other sufferers. That done, we can proceed to stronger measures. Only be guided by me, and obey all I tell you to do, and I promise you release and happiness."

Hilda promised and the brown bird took his leave. Next day he was no longer to be seen in the higher tree-tops, and after a week's absence, he arrived at nightfall dripping wet, and perched upon Hilda's window.

Carefully did Hilda collect every drop that fell from his plumage, and when next she followed the Grandmother of the Gnomes into the fatal crypt, it was with joyful footsteps, for in her hand she concealed a leaf-cup full of the elixir of life. Not even Hilda noticed that the little brown bird also entered the crypt when she did. On this occasion, she waited as usual to see the prisoners aroused and fed, then cast again into sleep; but instead of following the two crones on their return, she remained concealed in her crevice of the rock, and saw close upon her the doors of this living tomb. Now a sudden terror overtook her, and her knees trembled.

"Oh, dearest little bird, were you but by my side!" she whispered imploringly.

"I am here, Hilda," came in a well-known voice.

"Remember that all depends upon your courage and obedience. Go up to the crystal caskets and sprinkle a drop upon each in turn."

Hilda did so, and in a few moments had the inexpressible joy of seeing about twenty brave knights and other captives arise from their couches of marble. Last of all came her beloved father, who clasped her to his breast with rapture unspeakable.

"Now there is not a moment to be lost," said the brown bird, flying to Hilda. "Here, brave maiden, pluck the golden feather from my tail."

Hilda obeyed, and found that she held a shining sword within her hand.

"Quick, stab me to the heart!" said the bird.

Hilda burst into tears and pleaded with him to spare her; but the brown bird reminded her that, because of the water of life, he could never really die; so the young girl, trembling in every limb, plunged the blade into his breast.

As the warm blood rushed forth, a cloud of vapor arose, filling the cave; and blowing presently away, it revealed to all present the face and figure of a gallant youth, who, proud and smiling, knelt at Hilda's feet.

"Now is the enchantment banished!" he cried, as his

friends, recognizing their master, came flocking around him in delight. "But we must not again venture into the precincts of the gnome's garden, for who knows what might befall our lovely lady here? Come, my brave sword, point us a way of exit."

Swinging it in the air above his head, he brought the blade into a horizontal line in front of him. At once the sword pointed to a fissure in the walls of the crypt, and as the rescued band approached, it slowly widened to an opening through which a man might pass.

This was not a moment too soon, for the dwarfs on guard had discovered their attempt to escape, and a shrill whistle sounded in their ears. Swift as the lightning flash arrived the Grandmother of the Gnomes, this time in her worst aspect, fire darting from her eyes. Behind her came an army of angry little men in red, with hammers in their uplifted hands, prepared to do battle to the death. What was their fury to find the biers empty, and a long line of stalwart men, led by Hilda, escaping through a doorway in the solid rock! The last to depart was the prince, and advancing upon him with a horrible yell and glare of defiance came the Grandmother of the Gnomes. The prince met her with extended sword, and the enchanted blade pierced her to the heart. The frightened gnomes, surrounding their dead chief, laid her upon the marble slab from which Hilda's father had arisen, and then flew in pursuit of the avenger. But it was too late. The rocky wall had closed upon the retreating party, and the Grandmother of the Gnomes arose no more from her final resting-place.

The divining-sword led Hilda and her companions straightway to the surface of the earth, taking care, as they passed it by, to point out sufficient hidden treasure to enrich every man of the party. As for the prince, as he was already the owner of one of the richest kingdoms of the world, all he desired was to regain it, in company with his beloved Hilda, who by this time had pledged herself to be his bride. Hilda's father accompanied them to the palace of the prince, and was by him ennobled and enriched. The marriage took place, and just as the guests were enjoying the festivities, the new queen saw her servants turning away from the door a miserable-looking pair of beggar women. Bidding these pitiful creatures draw near to receive her alms, the queen recognized in them Dame Martha and her daughter. Such was the generosity of her nature, that Hilda could not resist disclosing herself to them, and assuring them that the *accident* of her fall had been the means of securing her wonderful good fortune.

She ordered fine clothes and fine rooms to be prepared for the couple, and would have forgiven them entirely, but that her father and the prince, interfering, ordered the wicked schemers to be driven from the house and kingdom.

Some time after, Dame Martha and Margaret re-appeared in the neighborhood of their old home. They were very sullen and close-mouthed, and were last seen hovering around the mountain-side in the direction of the old stone quarry, after which they were lost to human view.

The facts in the case are that Dame Martha's envy of her step-daughter led her to the desperate resolve to herself descend into the pit in company with her amiable child. Upon reaching the dwelling of the late Grandmother of the Gnomes, they were immediately seized and made to do duty in the cellar with the toads, mice, serpents, owls, and bats, where in all probability they are still enjoying life in congenial companionship.

DAME MARTHA'S STEP-DAUGHTER.

Hilda and her prince lived a long and happy life. The bright sword hung unused upon the wall, as no enemies appeared against whom to unsheath it, and the prince never again felt tempted to risk a visit to the kingdom of the gnomes.

Ha'penny Watching the Witch in the Underground Garden.

THE ADVENTURES OF HA'PENNY.

OR,

THE DWARF, THE WITCH, AND THE MAGIC SLIPPERS.

ONCE upon a time lived a poor, little, crooked dwarf named "Ha'penny." When he was born he was so small that his nurse exclaimed, "Why, he is no bigger than a ha'penny!" and thus the nickname settled upon him, as ugly nicknames often do upon very worthy people. His father was not very kind to the unfortunate child, who, finding himself pitied and avoided by children of his own age, soon learned to go off to the woods alone, and to spend the days with birds and animals, over whom he had extraordinary power. The most beautiful birds of many-colored plumage would flutter away from their boughs in the forest to perch upon Ha'penny's finger, and take sugar from his lips; shy little brown squirrels would scamper down the trunks of the great trees to nestle against his cheek; bees buzzed around his head without offering to sting him; pretty striped snakes glided from under their stones and stumps at his call; while all horses, and cows, and dogs, and cats loved to rub against him, and let themselves be stroked and petted at his will. This friendship with the world of animals and insects was Ha'penny's greatest joy, and during the summer time, when he could live abroad, the little creature was happy enough, after his fashion. In winter he had to content himself with feeding the birds, and visiting the stables to hide in the hay of the horses' manger, where the grooms would find him, mouthing and chattering in an unknown tongue. They would often scold him, and put him out of the stable, for Ha'penny was no favorite with his father's people. His mother had died when Ha'penny was a little fellow of five, and when he reached the age of fifteen (although looking much younger) his father married a second wife, who proved a cruel step-mother.

"If that ugly, little, twisted fright were out of the way, I could really enjoy life," the unkind woman would say to herself; and she lost no opportunity to make Ha'penny's life a burden to him, by all sorts of petty tricks and persecutions.

He bore all in silence, creeping away to his attic bedroom, and lying for hours on the floor sobbing bitterly. His only comfort was in his pets, and a queer lot they were. Among them were a dog, who had had both fore-paws cut off by the mowing-machine, a chicken with a cork leg, a blind cat, a land-terrapin, a dozen white mice, a number of birds which he had rescued from freezing and starvation, some trained fleas, a squirrel that had lost its tail—everything that was maimed, or homeless, or unfortunate. These he treasured in a little empty chamber opening out of his, and no one but himself ever approached it. All the poor dumb creatures loved him, and would swarm around him when he opened the door; and, in return, he spent upon them all the passion of love he had never bestowed on any one of his own kind.

One day when Ha'penny had gone off to the woods to search for some ripe partridge-berries for his birds, the step-mother found her way to his hidden menagerie. One instant she looked about her, with disgust and fury in her face, and then calling her maids she gave them cruel orders. Ha'penny came in from his walk, opened the door of his treasure-house—and alas! what a sight met his eyes! In two corners of the room hung his pet dog and cat, his terrapin was crushed under a heavy piece of iron, his birds were dead, his chicken's head was cut off, his mice were drowned in a pail; not one living thing remained to greet him but the trained fleas, who had taken refuge in the rafters overhead after biting the wicked mistress and her maids until they capered about in their misery!

Ha'penny gave one glance at his beloved pets thus wantonly sacrificed, and fell upon the floor sobbing with helpless rage and despair. He lay there all day without being inquired for, and when night came he stole out to the orchard and buried his poor dead favorites under the light of the stars. He would not go back to the house, and, forgetful of cold, hunger, everything but his burning sense of wrong, he wandered away, away, into the forest. A few berries and a crust he had carried for the birds were his only food until the evening of the next day, when he came in sight of a queer little hut, half hidden from observation by the trees that grew over it. Starving and desperate, Ha'penny was gaining courage to knock at the door. All at once a little lattice window opened, and an old woman poked her head out saying :

> "Come and eat, the table's spread
> With sweetest milk and whitest bread.
> Good cheer, enough for all I've got,
> And more is cooking in the pot."

At this Ha'penny pricked up his ears and licked his chaps like a hungry cur ; and just then a number of handsome cats and dogs came running out of the woods and toward the cottage door, which the dame had by this time opened. As no animal ever avoided Ha'penny, these creatures all fawned upon him, refusing to go in ; and the dame, perceiving the new-comer, asked him, with an angry air, what was his business.

"A little food and shelter, madam," said poor Ha'penny, the tears running down his cheeks.

"Begone, you rascal!" cried the angry woman ; "I don't believe a word you say. I believe you are a spy sent here to tempt away my pets. See how they hang around you. You must be a magician, for in general they will have nothing to do with strangers. Get you gone, sorcerer !"

Ha'penny turned meekly away, but the dogs and

cats followed him with every show of affection. Faint with hunger as he was, his legs tottered under him, and he soon fell to the ground. Then the cats and dogs surrounded him, licking his face and hands in spite of all their mistress's endeavors to coax them away.

The old woman's anger ceased when she found the grotesque-looking little stranger had really fainted from exhaustion. She lifted him in her arms and carried him in to the fire, and rubbed his cold limbs, putting spoonfuls of hot broth between his lips. By and by, when Ha'penny came to himself, he told her all his sad story, and when he reached the part about the killing of his pets, his heavy eyes flashed fire.

"She is a horrible wicked woman!" he exclaimed.

The dame answered by striking her staff on the floor. "See here, boy, if you are honest, you may stay here and mind my animals."

She took him into the next room, and there—what a funny spectacle! Twelve cats and twelve dogs lay upon cushions before the fire. The cushions were made of satin, and the covers were of velvet worked in gold. Twenty-four silver bowls stood in a row, and every cat or dog had its separate comb and brush, and bath-tub and towels, and sponge and soap, and perfume bottle, on a shelf. In the middle of the room played a fountain of rose-water, and at the windows hung pink silk curtains, which were drawn when the creatures went to sleep. All in this room was rich and costly, while the dame's own quarters were as plain as those of any other cottager. *She* was content to sleep in a big feather bed, to be covered by a clean patchwork quilt, to eat on a deal table off blue crockery, with a well-scoured pewter spoon. Ha'penny's eyes sparkled at the idea of waiting on the cats and dogs. He made friends with them at once. The dame gave him a clean bedroom under the roof, and every day after feeding and combing his charges he took them for a walk in the woods.

"So long as you wait on my darlings faithfully, and mind your own business," the dame said, "no trouble will come to you. But on no account ever go near the little closet in the peak of the roof. Should you do so, evil will happen, and your life may pay the forfeit."

Ha'penny suspected from this that his mistress was a witch; but it troubled him very little, as he was an honest lad and intended never to disobey her.

One day the dame brought home a new cat, a large, white Angora, a beauty to look at, with pink eyes and flowing hair, fine and silken as spun glass. From the moment of that cat's arrival the happy family was completely upset. Félisette, for so she was named, proved to be vain, selfish, and greedy; she fought for the best of everything, ate up her neighbor's bowl of milk as well as her own, and actually bit and spit at Ha'penny. Félisette soon became jealous of Ha'penny's affection for the others, and determined to do him an evil turn. One day the dame was going to the Witches' Sabbath, and said to Ha'-Penny, "Now mind and take especial care of my lovely darling, Félisette. If she gets into any trouble I shall hold you to answer for it, as I see the dear creature is not your favorite."

The dame went off riding on a broom-stick, and Félisette invented a thousand spiteful tricks to make the time pass unpleasantly to the others. At last she disappeared, and presently Ha'penny heard her crying pitifully upstairs. He rushed to see what was the matter, and discovered her with her tail caught in the door of the forbidden closet, up in the peak of the roof. She seemed about to die of the pain she was suffering, and, eager to set her free, the kind lad, without a moment's hesitation, lifted the latch while stroking Félisette's fur, when lo! as the door flew open, out came a skeleton hand, seizing poor Ha'penny in its grip! Up jumped Félisette, laughing heartily at the success of her trick, and ran away.

Ha'penny found himself held close in the embrace of two skeleton arms. In vain he struggled; the dreadful clasp only grew closer. He knew that this was a trap the witch had set to catch any one visiting the forbidden closet, so he made up his mind to die when his mistress should return. While he was in this sad way, the oldest of the dogs came up and licked his hands. Tears were running from

Ha'penny opens the magic closet.

its eyes, and to Ha'penny's great surprise the dog spoke.

"My poor friend!" said the oldest of the dogs, "I am afraid your fate is sealed. Know, then, that there is but one chance left for you to escape the witch's power. In this closet she keeps the magic slippers and the magic staff. Wearing the slippers, you may run faster than the wind; holding the staff, you may discover all the hidden treasures of the earth."

"But how can I get free of this horrible trap?" said Ha'penny.

The oldest of the dogs looked around to see that no one was listening, and then whispered:

"You must know that we twelve dogs were once twelve princes, and the twelve cats were princesses— all of us having turn by turn fallen into the power of the witch. She is bound to treat us according to our rank, but there is no hope of ever regaining human shape, I fear. Still, we may be able to help *you*, who have been so good to us."

He gave a little short bark, and up the stairs came running all the dogs and cats, who wept when they saw the sad plight of their friend. Up on a high shelf over the skeleton's head were the magic staff and slippers, and the thing was to get them down without touching the skeleton, which held fast every living thing that touched it. One of the cats ran nimbly up the wall and let herself hang; the next cat hung to her tail, and so on till a bridge was made, over which the oldest of the dogs scrambled, and got the coveted treasures. He put the staff in Ha'penny's hand, and fitted the slippers on his feet. Ha'penny gave a kick, and struck the ground with his staff. Instantly the arms of the skeleton relaxed their grip, and he was free. He bade a fond farewell to his dear friends, promising to come back to help them whenever he could. He set out to run from the house, and speedily the slippers carried him off at such a tremendous rate of speed that he was faint for want of breath. Vainly he tried to stop, but no; on, on he went with a fearful rush. He heard the cries of the old witch, who pursued him on her broom-stick. On, on, went poor Ha'penny, more dead than alive, and now the witch seemed gaining on him. He could hear the gnashing of her teeth. He struck out with his staff, as he passed by a rock, and instantly the rock became a mountain as high as the moon. The witch took some time to clamber over this, and meantime Ha'penny got far ahead of her. Reaching a city, he dashed into the midst of a funeral procession that was going through the street, and hid himself under the pall of the coffin, kicking off the slippers as he did so. Immediately he could walk as other men do, and when the old witch arrived she saw nothing but the funeral creeping slowly along—no sign of Ha'penny, who, hidden under the pall, clasped his magic slippers to his breast, and held tight to his magic staff. The disappointed witch flew homeward and whipped the cats and dogs soundly—excepting Félisette, who, of course, had been the telltale on poor Ha'penny.

The funeral train reached the cemetery, and Ha'penny thought it his duty to cry as bitterly as the rest of the mourners; but after the coffin had been put in the grave, and as they were turning away, he asked a bystander whose funeral it was.

"The king's messenger, to be sure, you simpleton," said the man.

"Could I get the place?" asked Ha'penny.

"You, the king's messenger!" said the man, scornfully. "Why, he must be the swiftest runner in the country. Look at your cork-screw legs! Look at your hump-back and your big head! As well expect a snail to carry our king's messages."

Nothing daunted, Ha'penny went to the king's chamberlain, and proffered his request. The chamberlain laughed until his head nearly dropped off, and then called the first Goldstick-in-waiting, who called the second, and soon the whole court was roaring over the absurd request of this poor mannikin to be the king's messenger.

"All I ask is that you try me," said Ha'penny, stoutly holding his ground.

"Stop! An idea occurs to me," said the jolly chamberlain, holding his aching sides. "To-morrow we shall have a running-match between this champion and the swiftest runner of the kingdom. In truth, my lords, this will be sport worth having," and he looked around at the courtiers, who all set to laughing anew.

Next day the match was held in a lovely grassy field. On a green mound in the centre was pitched a white satin tent, under which sat the king and queen and their children. An immense crowd assembled. Two bands of music kept playing all the time; there were free Punch and Judy shows on the outskirts of the crowd, and booths where lemonade was given away, with peppermint sticks and molasses taffy, to all who asked for it. Banners waved, trumpets blew, and then the race began. Side by side with Ha'penny, little and insignificant and forlorn as he was, started the king's swiftest runner, a man of beautiful light form and splendid muscle. Once around the field they ran, the dwarf lagging; but on the second round Ha'penny settled his feet well in his magic slippers, when, see! like an arrow he sped past the athlete, and was in at the goal so easily that the spectators hardly had time to wink their astonished eyes! Hurrah! hurrah! A mighty cheer went up for the successful Ha'penny, and the king called him to receive the purse of gold, which was the prize. Ha'penny knelt at the king's feet, and again asked to be made his messenger.

"That shall you be, my mannikin!" said the pleased monarch. So Ha'penny had a gold chain round his neck, a fine velvet coat to wear every day, and a page to serve his meals. The king grew so fond of his new servant that the rest of the courtiers became jealous. Soon Ha'penny again had no friends but the animals around the palace. They, as usual, followed him everywhere, and caressed him fondly.

Once when the little dwarf was walking in the king's

paddock, accompanied by a train of young deer who loved to be near him, he felt the staff in his hand give a loud thump on the ground. At the same time all the deer formed in a circle round the spot, seeming by their eyes to implore Ha'penny to remain there. At first he could not understand this, but at length occurred to him what the oldest of the dogs had said about hidden treasure. Ha'penny had no spade to dig with, but at once the deer went to work with their hoofs, and soon they had made a deep hole, at the bottom of which lay a large iron ring fastened to an iron door.

Ha'penny was not strong enough to pull this up; but the magic staff, when passed through the ring, lifted it easily. Below was a flight of steps, leading to a gallery. Ha'penny went down the steps, followed the windings of the gallery, and reached a second door. Touching this with the magic staff it yielded, and flying open disclosed to view a lovely garden, where roamed all sorts of strange shapes—men's and women's bodies bearing the heads of bears, lions, wolves, foxes, dogs, cows, horses, and cats. Instantly these creatures came flocking around Ha'penny, calling him their deliverer, and telling him that they too were victims of the witch, although by an accident she had only had time to change their heads before her spell expired. To this garden the witch was in the habit of coming once a week, to see how her victims were getting on, and to-day was the day of her visit. Ha'penny took the magic slippers from his pocket and put them on; and keeping firm hold of his trusty staff he hid behind a lilac-bush.

Soon, in came the witch, riding her broom-stick. Ha'penny had never before seen her in her true witch dress. It was a black, tight-fitting gown, made of scaly snake-skin, and she had a necklace of live coals. Around her high-peaked cap were twined two living serpents, and a toad formed her brooch. Under one arm she carried her familiar spirit, in the likeness of a black cat, with a single emerald eye. She wore a mantle, made of cobwebs and studded with large venomous red spiders. Oh! she was a terror to look upon, and no mistake! Ha'penny's teeth chattered with fear, and so would yours at sight of her! She rode sweeping her broom down the garden path, and instantly all the animals with human bodies came running to do her homage. She made them kneel before her, and, with the three-thonged whip of live snakes she carried, whipped them all cruelly, till they groaned and cried for mercy. Then, feeling tired, she lay down on a bank to sleep, guarded by her familiar, who kept watch with its single eye of flame; and on closely observing the horrid creature Ha'penny made no doubt that it was none other than his enemy, Félisette, in her rightful shape.

When the witch was fairly snoring, Ha'penny crept up behind, and summoning all his strength prepared to smite her with his staff. Suddenly the black cat spit and hunched her back. The serpents around the witch's hat began to writhe and uncoil. They knew an enemy was near.

Ha'penny saw that he must lose no time, so aiming a fierce blow at the witch's back, he broke her spinal column, just as you would break a stick of sugar-candy. Then the dying witch uttered a shrill command to her watchers, and instantly Félisette and the two serpents set upon the audacious Ha'penny. "This time you shall not escape me!" cried Félisette, spitting fire. The cat's breath was deadly poison, and the serpents' fangs no man might feel and live. Ha'penny struck, swift and sure, right into the middle of the cat's single eye, and pierced her brain. As Félisette fell dead beside the groaning witch, the serpents reared their full length from the ground, and prepared to strangle the dwarf. The good staff proved true, and cut them both in two with a single well-aimed blow. What was his horror to find the mangled remains of the snakes change into four living ones, stronger than the first. There was nothing for it but flight, and Ha'penny took to his heels. The magic slippers carried him on and away, so swiftly that nothing could catch him. He passed through the gallery and went out at the iron-door, finding himself safe, but a little out of breath, in the paddock with the king's deer.

Ha'penny told nobody of this exciting adventure, but could not sleep for thinking of all the poor bewitched people down there in the underground garden in the power of those dreadful snakes. He now suspected that these two fighting serpents were of the multiplication variety. (This means that if they were cut in two they would become four, from four become eight, from eight sixteen, from sixteen thirty-two, and so on indefinitely; and this, we are told, is the very worst species of snake known to travellers!)

Ha'penny got up early, went out again to the paddock, and found the deer in a great state of excitement and agitation. They seemed to be waiting for him to come, and led the way to the secret passage in the earth. Ha'penny went down, staff in hand, and easily passed through the first iron door. As he neared the second door, he heard a confused noise beyond it of cries and lamentations. He opened the door softly, and crept into the garden unobserved. There he saw the dying witch, who, as witches always require twenty-four hours to die in, was lying on the ground writhing horribly, groaning, and shrieking to her snakes to multiply, which they did until almost the whole garden was one seething, wriggling mass of the horrible creatures. The poor people in the garden had climbed up the trees, and were every moment expecting to fall to the ground poisoned by the breath of the serpents, which rose in a thick vapor.

In this terrible moment Ha'penny's heart almost failed him; but, mustering all his courage, he sprang upon the witch, and tore from her the mantle of cobwebs, to which he noticed she was clinging. Instantly the witch set up a shrill shriek.

"Give me back my mantle," she cried pitifully; "if I die with that around me, I can be sure of rest in the grave. If you take it away, I shall have to fly about like a bat forever."

"If you order the snakes to shrivel up and die, and restore all your victims to their natural shapes, I will give you the mantle," said Ha'penny firmly.

"Children, come home!" cried the witch, in a failing voice. Immediately the snakes began rolling and gliding into each other, and in a short while nothing was left but the two fiery serpents, who wreathed themselves quietly around the witch's hat again, as if nothing had occurred.

"Children, be dust!" she said again—this time in a weaker voice—and the snakes curled up and fell away, leaving behind them only two little shining skins.

"Be once more men and women, you accursed things!" she said spitefully, making a sign at the transformed beings who were now flocking around Ha'penny with delight and gratitude. As the witch spoke, the ugly deformities melted away, and in their place were seen the heads of handsome men and beautiful women, who wept for joy when they found themselves restored.

Ha'penny now threw the cobweb mantle over the witch, who, clutching it in her arms, gave one long shudder and expired. They made a grave for her then and there; and Ha'penny led his companions out of the magic garden, which they were glad to leave, into the long passage-way. There they showed him caverns filled with gold and silver, which it had been their business to dig out of the earth and to pack away for the witch. Ha'penny and his friends divided the spoil, although they told him it was all his by right. When they got up into the light of day once more, the bewitched people scattered in all directions to go to their various homes, and Ha'penny was again alone in the world, although now very rich. He persuaded the king to discharge him from the royal service, and his first thought was to journey to the cabin in the woods. This, by aid of the magic slippers, he did in very quick style, and there he found the twelve dogs and the twelve cats living as before. This distressed Ha'penny, as he had hoped that the breaking of the witch's spell would set them also free. "What did I tell you?" said the oldest of the dogs sadly. "We are doomed *never* to regain our shapes; but, now that Félisette has gone, we are comfortable here and don't repine. Only, there *should* be somebody to cook for us, and our hair has not been decently brushed for a week."

Ha'penny felt a sudden thrill of joy. Here, at last, was something to depend on him, something that he might live and care for. He warmed the water forthwith, and gave all the dogs and cats a bath apiece, and then he combed and brushed them nicely. He made the fire and heated their broth, and fetched fresh cream and white bread for their breakfast. Nothing was heard but little barks and purrs of enjoyment. Ha'penny waited till all were asleep on their cushions, and then he mounted the stairs and nailed up the skeleton cupboard, so that it might never again be opened. He could not take it quite away, you see, as every one must have a skeleton of some kind in his closet, and this was the only one he had. Ha'penny had never felt so happy and lighthearted as now. He had found friends, and might remain alone with them in peace.

So there he continued to live, and I am almost sure that if you would visit that forest, you might, even now, succeed in finding the cottage, the cats, and Ha'penny himself!

SYBILLA, MYRTILLO, AND FURIOSO.

 CERTAIN king had a beautiful golden-haired daughter named Sybilla, whose suitors came from every country, though with small success, since the princess had vowed to remain single until one proving to be the mightiest hero of the world should appear.

At no great distance from her father's country lived a horrible giant, every hair of whose head could change, at will, into a fiery serpent. He had one eye, the size of a mill-wheel, and his teeth looked like rocks in a mighty cavern. His name was Furioso, and his strength was known to surpass that of an army of ordinary men. What was the dismay of Sybilla's father when this monster sent to request the lovely princess for his wife! The king turned pale, and walked up and down his palace floor all night, for he knew what it meant to refuse the request of Furioso, who, up to this time, had lived at peace with his neighbor's country. The queen-mother, hearing of the giant's offer, took to her royal bed in kicking hysterics. As to the proud little princess, she curled her pretty red lips scornfully and tossed her head. "I'd like to see him do it, the fright!" was what she said.

In a few days what the king feared had come to pass. The giant Furioso, on receiving the beautiful diplomatic letter the king's secretary had written him (after consultation with all the lords and lawyers of the realm), frowned, scratched his head, which instantly bristled all over with flaming serpents, and opening his mouth sent forth a blood-curdling yell of defiance that resounded in the farthest part of the king's dominions. Without a moment's delay he changed himself into a fearful hurricane, and swept over the country and the palace of the Princess Sybilla. Fences and iron gates, stone walls and marble palaces fell to the ground like card-houses. Forests were uprooted, suspension bridges snapped like cobwebs, villages entire rose up into the clouds and disappeared, with their inhabitants looking in astonishment out of the windows! Cows and horses, dogs and elephants were seen whirling about in the air like Japanese day-fireworks. The king and queen found the roof lifted from above their heads, and went sailing out the open space in their nightcaps. They met all the court blowing wildly about up there, and for some time it was like a mad dance without any bottom to it. Dizzy and terrified, the royal couple at last fell down to earth again, the queen lighting on the fat cook, so that she was not seriously injured—the king falling on a tennis net, which the force of the wind kept suspended like a hammock without any ropes.

Picking themselves up, the first thought of the royal couple was for their beloved princess. As fast as different members of the court and household fell down from the clouds, which they continued to do all the evening and night, the king sent them in search of the princess. Nobody remembered having seen Sybilla anywhere in the air, and her waiting-maid, who dropped somewhere about nine o'clock A.M., next day, wept as she told how she was combing the princess' golden hair with the ivory comb she still held in her hand, when the breeze came which separated them. One thing was certain, the princess had disappeared. When things settled down a little, and people began taking

their breath, a peasant turned up who reported seeing the princess flying along at a fearful rate of speed in the arms of a tall, white-haired man wrapped in a mantle, who hid his face as he passed. "It were just at that moment, your honors," said the peasant, overwhelmed by the questions that rained on him, "I were myself tooken, unexpected-like, and turned upside down by the wind; and when I cum to, there I were a-top a haystack in Farmer Grimes' field, five miles from home as the crow flies, a-standing on my head."

The king and queen exchanged horrified glances.

Each remembered to have heard that one of the tricks of Giant Furioso, when he wished to be particularly wicked, was to change to the semblance of a venerable white-haired man. No doubt about it, the whole calamity to court and nation was the work of Furioso, and *he* had got the princess.

The distracted king set out at the head of his army to visit Furioso's castle. To his surprise, under the giant's name, upon a visiting card inserted above the speaking-trumpet at the gate, were pencilled these words: "Out of town till further notice." The windows were closed, and green shades hung behind them. No smoke came out of the chimneys, and the doors were chained. Evidently the giant had retired to some one of his retreats, where he could not be followed. The king and his army marched back again in gloomy silence.

For six months nothing was heard of the unfortunate Sybilla, till one day three young princes, travelling from a distant country in search of adventure, found a wounded carrier-pigeon on the road. Under its wing was a note, written in pale red ink, on a bit of torn linen cambric. The note gave them considerable trouble to read it, but, at last, the youngest prince, Myrtillo, who had always been the cleverest at school, managed to decipher these words:

"I write this with blood taken from my finger, on a fragment of my only pocket-handkerchief. I am the wretched Princess Sybilla, daughter of the King Rolando, and I pray any kind mortal who finds this to come to my aid, in the dungeon of Furioso, under the fifth mountain of the Impassable Range. Once in twenty-four hours this mountain cleaves asunder to let my oppressor take the air. Watch, and rescue me, in the name of humanity."

The Impassable Range was far away, but the princes journeyed thither without delay. They found the fifth mountain easily, and hid under the rocks at its base, to await developments. Exactly at sunrise a rumbling sound was heard, and the cliffs shook. The mountain split apart from summit to base, and between two yawning jaws of rock issued forth, first, a head covered with flaming serpents, then a frightful purple face, and lastly, the gigantic form of Furioso. Following him came the wails and shrieks of his captives within the mountain, to which Furioso paid no attention; he only turned his back and shouted:

> "Close you, mountain, fierce and grim,
> Open but to Banbedrim!"

The princes fancied that this last was the password, and when the giant had disappeared they tried to make the mountain open by repeating it; but in his excitement each one forgot how to pronounce the magic syllables. So there they stayed till sunset, when the giant came home from his hunting expedition. He had a pouch slung over his shoulder, and in it were crowded the new men, women, and children he had caught. The poor creatures were half dead with terror and rough treatment. The princes watched the giant, and listened with all their ears for the password. "Banbedrim!" thundered Furioso, and instantly the mountain yawned to let him and his miserable prisoners pass in, when it closed, as before.

The three princes laid each his hand on his sword, and swore to be avenged of the brutal treatment of their fellow-beings. Next morning when the giant issued forth, hurling the password at the mountain, then disappeared from sight, the oldest prince declared that he should be the first to enter the mountain, that his brothers should wait twenty-four hours for his reappearance, and that should he fail to come back the second brother might come to his assistance.

Bravely the young man sprang up the mountain-side, and called aloud the password. Instantly amid thunderings and lightnings the ground split at his feet and swallowed him from sight. They could see the tip of his bright sword held aloft, as he sank into the gloomy abyss.

Twenty-four hours passed, and the oldest prince failed to return. Then the second brother set forth, and he, too, vanished from sight. A long day and night of waiting had the youngest prince. Then he ascended the mountain where there was every reason to fear his brothers had found a horrible fate. Uttering the password, Myrtillo saw, through the opening earth at his feet, a pit whence came fire and smoke; and he plainly heard the cries for help of many human voices.

Myrtillo fell a great distance, landing on his feet in a desolate cavern. The smoke cleared away and he beheld a huge iron door before which were four trumpets—one of copper, one of silver, one of gold, and one of brass. Over them these words: "He who would enter here, choose between us four."

At the foot of the golden trumpet lay the mangled

remains of his oldest brother, who had perished in trying to blow it. At the foot of the silver trumpet the corpse of the second prince had fallen; and now Myrtillo must choose between the two remaining trumpets! Without a moment's hesitation he put his lips to the copper trumpet, and gave a loud, clear blast. At once the iron door flew open, and he was in a hall surrounded by dungeons, through whose gratings he could see prisoners in every stage of misery. They called to him frantically, and hailed him as their deliverer. Alas! what could the poor prince do to save them. He looked about and saw a long tunnel, ending in a massive gate of stone and iron. As he gazed into the darkness of the tunnel something coiled up at the end of it seemed to stir, and a hideous snake darted toward him, opening a pair of jaws as wide as an ordinary fireplace, and sending out a flaming tongue. Myrtillo charged upon the beast, and after a desperate fight drove his sword down its throat, the point coming out at the back of the neck. As he stooped to free his sword the serpent gave a convulsive struggle and died. Myrtillo found a chain around its neck on which was fastened a golden key. He took the key and put it in the great keyhole of the iron door before him, and to his joy the door opened. There, in a dismal dungeon within, lay a beautiful maiden in chains. Myrtillo set her free, and found that she was the Princess Sybilla, whom the giant treated with especial cruelty because she persisted in refusing his love. She told him that the little pigeon was one of many kept for the serpent's food, and that she had hidden it, and helped it to fly out one day when the giant left her cell. "And now," said the princess, when Myrtillo had in turn told her his story, "let us be quick, and lose no time. In the court beyond my cell are two fountains. One of them contains the water of strength, the other the water of weakness. From the former fountain Furioso gains all his power. A little of its water sprinkled upon the dead recalls them to life, and we may save your poor brothers yet."

Myrtillo and the lady hastened to the fountains; but to their dismay a roaring noise and the groans of the wretched prisoners, who were chastised daily upon his return, announced the arrival of the giant. "Quick!" said the lady, pointing to the water of strength; "drink once of this, and you will be strong enough to change the fountains, putting each in the place of the other."

Myrtillo obeyed, and at once felt able to move a mountain at command. He seized the solid stone basins and changed them, and hardly had he done so when the giant came rushing in. "Where is that insolent whipper-snapper of a prince who has dared to kill my faithful serpent?" roared he.

"Here he is, at your service," said Myrtillo, stepping forth with a gallant bow, and holding his glittering sword in hand.

"Just wait till I quench my thirst," said the giant disdainfully, as he stooped down to what he supposed to be his fountain of strength, and drank a long, deep draught. Suddenly a strange trembling came over the monster's huge bulk. His face turned pale, his eyes stared, his jaw dropped, he sank to the ground.

"Why, this is the water of weakness my prisoners drink," he cried. "What trick have you been playing me, you scoundrel?"

Myrtillo again drank of the water of strength, and now he felt as if he could defy an army, single-handed. Swift as a lightning flash he descended upon the giant, and severed his wicked head from his body. The Princess Sybilla uttered a wild shriek of delight, which was heard and understood by all her fellow-captives, and the dungeons echoed with sobs and cries of joy. Myrtillo and the princess filled goblets with the water of strength, and hastened to sprinkle all the prisoners, who, paralyzed by their chains and wasted with hunger, could in many cases barely stir upon the ground where they lay. Soon, a host of strong men and women filled the main hall of the dungeon, and then Myrtillo had the joy of seeing his two brothers return to life under the action of the magic water, in which he bathed their limbs. As Myrtillo only had *drank* of the water of strength, he remained the strongest champion in the world; and when Sybilla was taken back to her father and mother, she told them that she had promised to take the Prince Myrtillo for her husband. From the giant's stronghold Myrtillo brought away gems and gold enough to enrich him for a lifetime, even after all the giant's victims had been sent home with a bag of gold apiece. His brothers found brides in two lovely fellow-sufferers they had led out of the giant's cavern to the light of day; and so all were satisfied, and in a short time the Giant Furioso was forgotten. No more hurricanes visited the kingdom of Sybilla's father, where things continued to jog along in the old-time peaceful fashion.

ANNETTE; OR, THE MAGIC COFFEE-MILL.

A POOR woman and her daughter, who were on the verge of starvation, saw a little green bud of a plant growing through their cottage floor. They watered it, and in a day or two it sent forth long shoots, and became a vine, fine and delicate to look at, but tough as an iron wire. The vine put forth leaves, soon covering the inner walls of the cottage. The tendrils waved longingly toward the sun, and so the mother and daughter set their lattice window open, when, lo! the vine escaped as if it had wings and grew quickly heavenward. Lovely flowers bloomed on it, in shape like morning-glories, and rare birds came to drink the honey of their chalices. The maiden leaned out of her window and looked up. Higher, higher climbed the vine, till it was lost in the blue sky above them. The girl was seized with a yearning desire to climb up and see what could be seen. Her mother gave her leave, and she set out. Up, up, she went, and the mother watched below till the clustering green and many-colored bells hid her child from sight. At last the girl reached a wonderful new country, and stepped off the vine upon a shining silver path, which she followed through a green meadow till she came to a house made of honeycomb that glittered, oh! so beautifully. The columns of the porch were sticks of lemon-candy, and there were little benches to rest yourself upon, made of maple-sugar and cushioned with gingerbread. Annette, for so the girl was called, ventured to open the door of the house and peep in. There she found more beautiful things than I can tell you of—toys and books and pictures—and all the furniture was made of cake with raisins in it, so that, if one sat down to read, one need only turn around and nibble a knob off the chair, or pick raisins out of the arm of the sofa. Annette played a little and read a story-book, then she fell asleep on a couch made of apple-dumplings. Suddenly in came three goats, who were the servants of the fairy to whom this house belonged. "Let us butt her to death," said the oldest goat. "Let us trample on her, and bite her," said the second goat. "Let her alone," said the third goat, who was a kind little fellow with golden horns. "If she holds her tongue, and if she don't find out the secret of the golden coffee-mill, our mistress will let her stay here and work for her."

Annette heard this while pretending to be asleep, and when the fairy came home, she jumped up and made a nice little courtesy, begging to be allowed to do the housework. "Well," said the fairy, after looking at her sharply, "I will try you; only don't undertake to grind my coffee for me, and don't gossip with the goats."

Annette lived there for six months, and learned to make all kinds of goodies; for the fairy was the queen's confectioner in that country. You might eat all you pleased, provided you didn't talk; and not a word spoke Annette, and not a word spoke the goats. Every day the fairy went into a pantry and there ground her coffee; and every day she carried two or three bags full of something heavy, and put them in her chariot, and drove off with them. The coffee-mill looked like any other one, and Annette wondered vainly what its secret was. At last curiosity overcame her, and she stole into the pantry and began to grind the mill. Down fell a stream of pure gold-dust, and it powdered Annette all over till she looked like a golden image. "How shall I get rid of this?" she said, trying to shake it off, but the gold dust stuck fast. She cried and sobbed, for she knew that now the fairy would certainly find her out. In came the friendly goat. "Cheer up," said he. "That was the way my horns came to be gilded, because I yielded to my curiosity about the mill, when I first came here to live. The fairy wanted to kill me, but she let me off when I vowed to serve her faithfully for seven years. The time is just up, and so I propose that we escape together. Take the magic mill under your arm and get upon my back, and we will go down to your world."

Annette joyfully obeyed the friendly goat, and carrying the coffee-mill they set off from the fairy's house. Unfortunately she did not know how to stop the mill from grinding, and it left a path of gold-dust behind them as they fled, which showed the way to the fairy. The fairy followed them, riding on a silver broomstick; but the goat was swift as the wind, and Annette clung to his golden horns, and held the magic mill tight under her arm. By good luck they reached the opening, near which the vine was growing, and, just as the furious fairy got near enough to stretch out her long arm after them, down went Annette, goat, and coffee-mill, through a rift in the clouds, to a land where their enemy could not follow them. The faithful vine caught them as they fell, and held them up stoutly. When they had climbed down, and touched the earth in safety, Annette was astonished to see her goat turn into a handsome young prince, with curling golden locks and kind blue eyes.

"You have freed me from my enchantment, beautiful maiden," he said, kneeling upon the grass at her feet. "Long years ago I and my wicked brothers were captured by the fairy and became her slaves under the form of goats, as you saw. For fear that they may find out some way to

follow us, we must cut down this vine, and then we shall be free forever from all dread of disturbance."

Annette's mother came running out, kissed her child, and listened with wonder to the tale of her adventures. All this while the mill had gone on grinding, and before they knew it the cottage floor was knee-deep in gold-dust. "We shall be smothered at this rate," cried the prince laughing, and he hastened to make a magic sign he had learned from the fairy. The mill ceased to flow, and then the prince took an axe and cut the beautiful vine at its root. Annette wept to see the lovely leaves and blossoms shrivel up, but in a short time they vanished entirely from sight. The prince married Annette, and every day the mill ground gold enough to pay all the expenses of their palace and servants and horses, and also the expenses of Annette's mother, who had a separate palace for herself over the way.

The country people, for years after the time when Annette and the prince came down the magic vine, showering gold-dust along their way, continued to talk about the wonderful rain of stars they had seen in the sky that moon-lit night.

JULIET; OR, THE LITTLE WHITE MOUSE.

ONCE upon a time there lived a king and queen who loved each other so dearly that they were an example to all the married couples in their kingdom. In an adjoining country lived a wicked king, who spent his life in envying the happiness of his neighbors. He was a sworn enemy to all good and charitable people, and his chosen companions were robbers and murderers. His air was stern and forbidding. He was lean and withered, dressed always in black, and his hair hung in long elf-locks over his fiery eyes. This wicked wretch, determined to end the happiness of his neighbor, raised an immense army and marched to attack the kingdom of the Land of Sweet Content, for so the good king's country was called.

The king of Sweet Content made a brave defence, but it was all in vain. The immense numbers of the adversary overpowered him and his troops. One day when his poor queen was sitting with her infant daughter in her arms, waiting for news from the battle-field, a messenger on horseback galloped up to the door, and entered the room where she was, with every sign of terror.

"Oh! madam," he cried, "all is lost. The king is slain, the army defeated, and the ferocious King Grimgouger is even now marching to take you prisoner."

The queen fell senseless on the floor; and while her attendants were making every effort to provide a means of flight for her and the little princess, the army of the foe, with banners flying and with music playing, marched into the city. Surrounding the palace, they called on the queen to surrender. No answer was given, and the horrid King Grimgouger instantly ordered a file of his most blood-thirsty soldiers to march through the palace and to kill everybody they met, except the queen and princess.

Now nothing was heard but shrieks and lamentations from the doomed attendants of the queen. When all were sacrificed, the tyrant Grimgouger walked into the apartment where the terrified queen stood, clasping her child in her arms, and prepared for death.

"You won't die now, madam," he thundered, seizing her by the long hair, and dragging her after him down the stairs and over the stones of the courtyard to his chariot. She was all bruised and bleeding, and knew nothing more till she found herself in a tower-room, where dampness dripped from the walls, and the light of day could scarcely reach through a small grated window. She lay upon a little heap of mouldy straw, and her child cried for food beside her, while over her stood a wicked fairy to whom King Grimgouger had given the prisoners in charge. The fairy threw her a few crusts without any butter on them, and the baby seized one eagerly, and stopped crying as she sucked it.

"That is all either of you shall have to-day," said the fairy. "To-morrow they will decide what to do with you. Probably you, queen, will be hanged, and your daughter be saved to marry the son of our good King Grimgouger."

"What! That ugly little reptile of a prince!" screamed the queen. "Hang me, if you will, but don't give my beautiful angel to a husband like that!"

"Then she, too, will be hanged," said the fairy, grinning maliciously, and flying away with a fizz of flame, leaving behind her the smell of sulphur matches.

Next day the fairy gave the queen three boiled peas, and a small bit of black bread, and the next, and the next, until the poor queen wasted to skin and bone, and the baby looked like a wax doll that had been left out in the rain all night.

"In a few days it will be over," thought the poor queen. "We shall be starved to death."

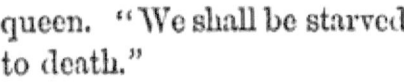

She fell to spinning with what strength remained to her (for the fairy made her work, to pay her board, she said), and just then she saw, entering at a small hole, a pretty little mouse as white as snow.

"Ah! pretty creature," cried the queen, "you have come to a poor place for food. I have only three peas, which are to last me and my child all day. Begone, if you, too, would not starve."

The little mouse ran about, here and there, skipping so like a little monkey that the baby smiled, and gave it the pea she had for her supper.

The instant she had fed the mouse, what was the queen's surprise to see, start out of the prison floor, a neat little table, covered with a white cloth, having on it silver dishes, containing a roast partridge, a lovely cake, some raspberry jam, and for the baby a big bowl of fresh bread and milk, with a silver spoon! How they did eat! I leave you to imagine it!

Next day the mouse came again, and devoured the queen's three peas, her whole day's supply. The queen sighed, for she did not know where anything else was to come from. She stroked the little mouse, and said gently, "Pretty creature, you are welcome." Immediately the same little table sprang up out of the floor. This time there was broiled chicken and ice-cream, green peas, marsh-mallows and custard, with a fresh bowl of bread and milk for the baby. "Oh! you dear little mouse," said the queen. "This must be your work! If you could only help me to get my baby out of this dreadful place, I would thank you forever."

The mouse ran up to her with some straws in its mouth. This gave the queen an idea, and taking them she began to weave a basket, for she was a clever queen, and knew how to use her pretty white hands in a variety of useful ways. The mouse understood her, and brought her more straws, until she had made a nice covered basket large enough to hold the baby. Then the queen cut her petticoat into strips, and plaited them, till she had a long and strong cord. She tied the basket to this, and wrapping the beautiful little smiling princess in the only covering she had, laid her in the basket, crying all the time as if her heart would break. Then she climbed up to the window, and (the little white mouse watching her with a very friendly air) looked down to see if she could attract the attention of any charitable person who might be passing in the street below.

There she saw an old woman leaning upon a stick and looking up at her.

"Pray, goody," said the queen, "have pity on an innocent babe, and save it from destruction. Feed and nurse her, and heaven will reward you, if I cannot."

"I don't want money," said the old woman; "but I am very nice in my eating, and I have a positive longing for a nice, little, fat, white mouse. If you can find such an one in your prison, kill it and throw it out to me. Then, right willingly, will I take your pretty babe and nurse it carefully."

When the queen heard this, she exclaimed to herself, "Oh! the dreadful old thing!" and began to cry. "There is only one mouse here, madam," she said aloud, "and that is so pretty and engaging that I can't find it in my heart to kill it, even to save my child."

"Hoity-toity!" said the angry old creature, thumping her stick on the ground below. "If you think more of a miserable little mouse than of your child, keep them both, and be hanged to you!"

So saying, her staff changed to a broom-stick, and with a fizz and a bang the old hag shot up into the sky like a rocket. And there was again a strong smell of sulphur matches in the air!

The queen, seeing that this was, without doubt, the wicked fairy come to try her, gave way to new grief. She kissed her hapless little one, and just then the mouse jumped into the basket. The baby's rough clothes changed to finest linen and lace, and a pillow of down was under her head, while a gay silver rattle was put into her hand.

More surprises! As the queen watched, the mouse's paws changed to tiny hands with jewelled rings upon them. The little face grew into the image of a smiling old woman's, and a figure of a pretty old-time fairy stood before her. As these fairies have been rather out of fashion lately, I will tell you just how she was dressed. She wore a chintz gown, looped up over a blue silk quilted petticoat. A lace ruff was around her throat, and her long-pointed bodice was laced with silver. Over her mob-cap she had a high sugar-loaf hat tied on with pink ribbons, and her feet were clad in the prettiest black silk stockings and high-heeled black satin slippers, with big diamond buckles. When you remember that she was just of a size with the baby princess, you will agree that you would have liked to see her.

"What is the baby's name?" said the fairy.

"Oh—Juliet; I thought I had mentioned it," said the queen, apologetically.

"I have never heard anything but 'pecious wecious,' and 'mother's blessing,' and things like that," said the fairy. You may stop crying now, for I will save Juliet. If you had given me to the wicked fairy, she would have gobbled me up in a minute, so you see I owe my life to you. Henceforth I will take Juliet under my protection. She shall live to be an hundred years old, and never have an illness or a wrinkle."

Fancy it, children! No mumps, no measles, no

whooping-cough, no castor-oil! What rapture in the thought!

The queen kissed the fairy's little hand, and begged that Juliet should at once be taken away. So the weeping princess was put into the basket, and carefully let down to the bottom of the tower. Then the fairy resumed the shape of a mouse and ran after her down the string, which the queen still held in her hands. Suddenly she came running back again. "Alas! alas!" she cried to the terrified queen, "our enemy, the fairy Cancaline, was hidden below, and seized upon the child, and flew away with it. Unfortunately she is older and more powerful than I am, and I don't know how to rescue Juliet from her hands."

At these words the queen uttered a loud cry, and in came running the jailer of the tower, his men, some soldiers, and after them, gnashing his teeth with rage, the horrid Grimgouger himself.

"Where is the child?" he said, stamping.

"Alas, I know not, king," said the mother. "A fairy has taken it off."

"Then you shall be hanged at once," he cried in a fury. "Seize her, guards."

They dragged the poor queen by the hair of her head to the gallows. Just as the executioner was about to tie the rope around her neck, the gallows fell down beneath him and knocked out all his front teeth, while invisible hands carried the queen through the air to a safe retreat in the mountains. She found herself in a beautiful castle, where all her attendants were white mice. Here the queen lived for eighteen years, surrounded by luxury and tender care. But she always thought of her little daughter, and dreamed of her by day and night. The mouse fairy made every attempt to find news of the lost princess, but failed to do so.

At this period the son of the wicked King Grimgouger had grown up, and everybody was talking about his strange fancy for a poultry-woman's maid-servant, who had refused to marry him in spite of his rank and fine clothes. The story went that the prince sent her, every day, a new gown of silk or velvet, and that the girl would not look at them. So the little white mouse fairy determined, through curiosity, to have a peep at this strange damsel. Accordingly she visited King Grimgouger's capital, and entering the poultry-yard found there an extremely beautiful young creature dressed in a coarse woollen gown, with her feet bare, and a cap of goat-skin on her head. Lying by her side were magnificent dresses, embroidered with gold and silver and ornamented with precious stones; the turkeys and other fowls that surrounded her trampled on them and spoiled them. The poultry-girl sat upon a stone in the yard when the king's son arrived; he was crooked, and humpbacked, and horrible to look upon.

"Do you still refuse to marry me, fair maiden?" he asked. "If so, I shall have you put to death immediately."

"I am not afraid of you, prince," the girl replied, modestly. "I certainly should prefer death to marriage with you. And I like the society of my chickens and turkeys better than yours, if it please your highness."

The prince went off in a rage, and the mouse fairy appeared, in her real shape as a little old lady.

"Good-day, fair damsel," she said. "I respect you and admire you—let me be your friend."

"Willingly, good madam," said the girl. "I am greatly in need of friends, as you may see."

"Have you, then, no father or mother, my child?"

"None, madam; I am an orphan, and this poultry-yard is my refuge from the cruelty of the only protector I have ever known. The fairy Cancaline, who had charge of me, used to beat me until I was nearly killed. Weary of suffering I ran away from her at last; and while wandering in a wood I met the prince, who promised to befriend me, and placed me here as poultry-girl. Alas! now that I find he is in love with me, I must leave this place, and where to go I know not."

"And what is your name, my dear?" asked the mouse fairy, affectionately.

"Juliet, madam."

"Then, kiss me, my dear; I knew you before you knew yourself," the fairy cried, joyfully. "I am delighted to see you so sensible. But your complexion is a little dark. Bathe in yonder fountain. And you should be better dressed. Put on one of these dresses, and then let me see you."

The girl obeyed. On taking off her cap of goatskin her long golden curls fell nearly to her knees. After bathing in the fountain she revealed a complexion more bright and transparent than the choicest pearls of India. Roses bloomed in her cheeks, and her eyes shone like the brightest diamonds. Her figure was light and graceful as a young fir-tree. The fairy gazed at her in wonder and delight. Her next thought was to restore the lost child to her mother.

"Stay here one moment," she said, "while I fly back to your mother, and prepare her for this happiness, lest she should die of joy."

The son of the wicked King Grimgouger went back to his father, and cried and groaned dreadfully. His boo-hoo might have been heard for miles, and the king naturally desired to stop it.

"What in the world are you roaring about?" asked the father.

"I'll roar as much as I like," said the spoiled prince. "If I can't marry the poultry-girl, I'll roar for a week without stopping."

"Good gracious!" cried the alarmed king; "guards, go and fetch her here at once."

The guards went to the poultry-yard, and found the princess Juliet, dressed in gorgeous attire, and looking more beautiful than the new moon.

"Whom do you seek, my good men?" she said in a soft voice.

"Madam," they answered humbly, "we are looking for a vile creature named Juliet; but you would never have stooped to notice her."

"I am she," the princess said, proudly.

Upon this the guards seized her, bound her hands and feet, and roughly carried her into the presence of the king.

"So you won't have my son, miss," shouted the king. "Don't love him, hey? Stuff and nonsense! Love! Gammon and spinach! Marry him at once, or I'll have you flayed alive! Here, you rascal (addressing his son, who had now roared himself quite black in the face), stop that racket, for goodness' sake, or you'll split my head."

But the princess held out firmly. They sent for a chaplain, but the princess said "no," instead of "yes," and when they shook her till she couldn't utter a syllable, she nodded her head from side to side. So, finding it quite a hopeless matter, the king ordered the prince put to bed with ice upon his head, and the princess to be shut up for life in a high tower, where she would never more see the light of day.

At this moment the good mouse fairy returned in her flying chariot, and with her was the queen mother, who was almost crazy with delight at the prospect of embracing her child. When they heard the sad fate of Juliet, the queen wrung her hands in agony; but the fairy bade her cheer up, as she would find a way to help the captive.

King Grimgouger had gone to bed in a rage, and the little white mouse ran up on his pillow. First she bit one ear, and made him turn over in his sleep. Then she bit the other, and made him turn back again. Now the king woke up, and howled for his attendants. They came running in, and while they sought to stanch the blood that flowed from his royal ears, the little white mouse ran to the chamber of the sleeping prince, and served him exactly the same way. The prince, who, to the great relief of the household, had fallen asleep in the very act of crying, now woke up and began again, this time with a vengeance.

"Confound that fellow, he's at it again," said the king, smarting from his wounds. "Stop him, somebody; and get me the court-plaster, and the arnica, and the Pond's extract, and the chloroform; and send for all the surgeons."

While the attendants ran hither and thither the mouse returned to visit the king. She bit his nose, and bit his toes, and bit his fingers; and when he opened his mouth to scold and yell, she bit a piece of his tongue off, so that he could not articulate, but could only make absurd mouthings, at which everybody wanted to laugh, yet dared not.

Then she ran back to the prince, and ate out both of his eyes, which sent him flying out of bed. He seized his sword, and ran storming and swearing into the apartment of his father, who, on his side, had taken a sword, and vowed to kill everybody around him if they did not catch the mouse who had done this mischief.

The prince could not understand what his father said, and as he was blind, attacked the king furiously. The king made a violent cut back at him, and in ten minutes they were in the thick of an awful fight, which ended in both being mortally wounded at exactly the same moment. Seeing them fall, their attendants, who hated the wicked tyrants, made haste to tie them hands and feet, and tumbled them into the swiftly flowing river.

Thus ended the horrible King Grimgouger and his son. The good fairy now took her own shape, and, leading the queen by the hand, opened the door of the tower where Juliet was confined. Juliet flew into her mother's arms, and all was happiness.

The kingdom of Grimgouger and that of Sweet Content, which he had joined to his, were now without a sovereign, and the people, by universal consent, chose Juliet to reign over them. Juliet became their queen, and in due time married a young king, who was rich and handsome, and wise and witty, and brave and modest—all that a young husband ought to be. The little white mouse continued to be their chief friend and counsellor.

Simon's Benefactor.

THE FAIRIES AND THE FIDDLER.

IN the pretty little village of Hayfield, not far from the borders of a thick forest, lived a good-natured, idle fellow, named Simon, who supported his wife and two children by trapping or shooting in winter, and by fishing or doing odd jobs of harvest work in summer. Simon could play upon the fiddle in a way to make the tears come into your eyes; or if he chose to be merry, his tunes would set every foot in motion, as the wind starts the leaves upon an aspen tree. This accomplishment caused him to be much in demand among the young people of the village, who dropped many a bit of silver into his worn old hat; and at all the weddings and barn-dances, Simon might be seen with a huge bunch of flowers in his buttonhole, and his fiddle under his arm, footing it in the procession. Then, too, Simon was the best man in the village to coax stories from, especially the old-time gossip about the little folk in green, for whom in former days Hayfield had been famous. Simon knew how the fairies dressed, what they ate and drank, how they punished saucy human beings who offended them; and could point out the smooth rings of short fine grass where they had held their midnight revels. That the fairies really had haunted Hayfield and its surrounding woods, nobody in the village doubted. They had heard too many things to prove it from their grandparents, whose parents were said to have lived on the best of terms with the little people—setting pans of cream by the hearth-stone at night for them to skim—leaving, when the holidays came around, a cheese and bag of nuts in a hollow tree at the entrance of the wood—and getting all sorts of kind offices from the fairies back again. Although it had now been a long time since any one could testify to having actually seen a fairy (as it was well known that the band were frightened out of Hayfield when the first stage-coach, with its noise and clatter, took to dashing along the village street), many people believed the men in green to be still lurking in the neighborhood. What else could account for the trouble some of the good wives had with their butter and their bees? What could it be but fairy thumps and pinches that kept the lazy folk from sleeping soundly, when their houses were not to rights before they went to bed. And what could explain the silver penny often found in the shoe of a tidy housekeeper, when up she jumped at break of day to set her maids to work? For fairies never show by day, and it is only when the people of a house are fast asleep and snoring, that they glide in by key-holes, through cracks and broken panes of glass, and swarm over the rooms, spying out  everything amiss, and leaving tracks on the dust of shelves or tables, scattering the ashes of an unswept hearth, and bewitching the inside of a dirty iron pot, so that it never more may cook sweet porridge!

Of all the villagers, as I have said, Simon alone professed to have any recent acquaintance with the little folk, and the wonder was how they, who were known to be sworn enemies to idleness, could keep him in their favor.

Simon's house was a poor little cottage on the outskirts of the town. His wife, once a pretty, rosy lass, had taken to drink, and the husband and children led a dog's life within doors. Consequently, their one pleasure was to roam the woods and fields, and the children were growing up brown and barefoot as two young gypsies. They were a boy named Timothy and a girl named Bess, of whom Simon was very proud, their fresh young faces making a strong contrast with his wizened visage, crossed with a hundred lines, and topped with a sunburned mop of hair. As they grew old enough to understand, their father instructed them in all the arts of woodcraft. There was no tree or plant for which he had not a name or a virtue. The habits of all birds and fishes and animals were as familiar to him as their haunts. In this way, the vast green forest, with its great tree-boles and twisted boughs, its verdant moss-carpet and hidden streams, became to them an enchanted world, through which the children strayed like a sylvan king and queen. A sad change it was to come back to the dirt and confusion of their miserable home, where the mother received them either with grudging welcome if they brought berries or a string of brook trout, or with blows and drunken curses if they came empty-handed. As his wife's intemperance increased, Simon stayed less and less at home, and the children dreaded lest some day their poor father would be driven to desert them altogether. So they resolved to keep a close watch on his movements, and to follow him should he go away.

One night the harvest moon was riding her glorious way across the heavens, and the little village of Hayfield lay steeped in silver light. Not a lamp or a taper glimmered in the hamlet, and every one of the brown thatched cottages was buried in profound repose.

Not even a watch-dog barked; and the forest-leaves yielded to the universal spell, and ceased to rustle.

There had been held a harvest-home that day, and Simon had been hard at work with his fiddle, playing jigs and reels for the dance in the squire's great barn. Between every dance, he had quenched his thirst at the cider-barrel, or quaffed the big brown mug of beer they kept brimming at his side. Naturally, Simon's brain was a little the worse for such free potations; and when the last strains of the "Wind that Shakes

THE FAIRIES AND THE FIDDLER. 113

the Barley" had died upon his fiddle-strings, and all the gay company had gone their homeward way, Simon with his pocket full of silver pennies staggered out into the field, and lay down under a haystack to take his well-earned rest.

There, just before midnight, his two children, who had come in search of him, found their father peace-

fully sleeping, his fiddle on his breast. Not wishing to disturb him, the children decided to have their own night's sleep in the same fragrant nest of hay; and curling up at some little distance from the slumbering fiddler, they whispered together for a while, and then were about to drop asleep. Just as their eyes were closing they heard an odd sound, as of hundreds of little pattering feet, and out from the shadow of the wood came into the unbroken argent of the field a long train of little men, women, and children, dressed magnificently in cobweb gauze and green, bespangled with glittering gems, and wearing each a tiny crimson cap with a golden bell upon its peak. The two children were broad awake in a moment, for they knew that these were the fairies they had so longed to see, all dressed in holiday costume, and proceeding to their famous midsummer festival. The procession wavered like a gleaming snake across the field, and, when passing near the haystack, came to a halt. To the children's surprise, two queer little old men, holding carved ivory wands, came straight up, and tapped the sleeping fiddler across the bridge of his nose.

"Nay, I will play no more for you, you light-of-head and light-of-heel," said sleepy Simon, believing himself to be still perched upon the barrel that served as the fiddler's throne.

"Aye, but play you shall, at his Majesty's command," said the little old man, thumping him more sharply. "Isn't that part of your bargain with us, if we allow the trout to haunt your brook, and the hares to run into your traps? Come, mortal! Up with you and follow. Here's the bandage to blindfold your eyes, as

THE FAIRIES AND THE FIDDLER. 115

usual; and remember that, if you peep, you are our prisoner for life."

By this time thoroughly awakened, Simon stumbled upon his feet, and stood making abject bows before the angry little fairy chamberlains. He let his eyes be bound with a green silk ribbon, and leading-strings were passed around his waist. At the blast of a golden trumpet, the procession moved forward with a sound of tripping feet and whirring gauzy wings and tinkling bells most lovely to the ear.

Last of all came Simon, in fairy leading-strings, and the two children, unable to resist the impulse, followed noiselessly.

Their way led again into the forest, through the dense underwood, to a smooth circle of velvet sward, set around with hundreds of little mushrooms, on which the fairies took their seats. In the centre was a hammock of silver cobweb, swinging by jewelled chains from the crossed stems of two tall white lilies, under a bower of maiden-hair ferns. Sweet blue violets were sprinkled in the grass, making a path where the king and queen of the fairies marched to take their places on the cobweb-throne. Dew was handed around in acorn-cups, of which the fairy guests sipped daintily, followed by bark trays containing every variety of fairy refreshment. There were delicate fried butterflies, marrow-bones of a field-mouse, snail soup served in nutshells, and wild strawberries in baskets made of moss.

When the banquet was at an end, the chamberlains gave notice to Simon, who had been bound with ropes made of plaited grass to the trunk of a wide-spreading oak; the fiddle struck up a tune, and at once the dance began. Such a mad and merry dance the wondering children had never seen before! Old and young joined hands and trod a circle, then, breaking the chain, formed into a hundred fantastic figures; and at each touch of a light footstep, the earth opened to give birth to a flower, until the entire fairy ring was enamelled with fragrant blossoms. Fast flew the fiddle-bow, but faster flew the tiny feet; and when the mirth was at its height, Simon who, as we know, had taken a drop too much, was suddenly inspired to tear the bandage from his eyes, and crying, "It's my turn now," capered right into the middle of the magic ring.

The honest fellow had meant no harm, but his offence was a mortal one!

Instantly, he was surrounded by a swarm of the

furious little men in green, who, without waiting for an excuse, stabbed out both his eyes, and taking away his fiddle and bow, bound his arms behind his back. Again the procession—this time sad and silent—was formed, and the king striking the nearest tree with his wand, it flew open; the whole party, leading Simon behind them, entered the aperture, and before the children knew where to turn, it had closed upon their father.

And now, in what a distressing condition were the unhappy Timothy and Bess! Not knowing what better to do, they sat down at the foot of the great oak-tree which had swallowed up their father, and from sheer weariness fell asleep. When morning came, and the birds piped upon the boughs, the children awoke and looked in wonder about them. All was dewy, green, and fragrant in the deep woods, but no sign remained of the fairy revel, except a fine fringe of newly sprung grass, growing in a circle where their ring had been.

The bark of the great oak tree was unbroken, and above stretched a broad canopy of dark-green leaves, which whispered in the morning breeze, but told no tales of what the children longed to know. Hunger drove them to retrace their steps homeward; and when they reached the cottage, their mother was so cross at her husband's failure to fetch her the usual stock of silver pennies earned at the harvest-home, that she beat them both soundly, and gave them but a dry crust apiece for breakfast.

Still the children hoped their father might return; and, not knowing to whom to confide their wonderful tale, they kept silence. When it was found Simon had disappeared in earnest, all the wise heads in Hayfield decided that he had run away to escape from his good wife's tongue, an act of independence which had the bad effect of making more than one married man in the village unduly restless.

A month passed, and the two children were again wandering in the forest trying to find a few berries to appease their hunger (for things at home were now worse than before), when they fancied they heard a child crying close at hand. They searched everywhere, and at length the sound was renewed, seeming to come from a thicket of tall ferns. Falling on their knees, the children worked their way under the bushes and through the brakes, until they came in view of a lovely chubby elf sitting forlorn upon a mushroom on a hillock of soft green moss, beneath a screen of ferns and wild flowers, and letting fall a flood of tears from his big blue eyes. He wore no clothing, if we may except a pair of drooping wings, and in his hand he held a stalk of snowy lilies.

"Who are you, dear little one, and how came you here?" they asked.

"I am a fairy," the tiny creature sobbed. "Last night was the monthly revel, and we sported till the moon set. But I saw these lilies growing over in yonder swamp, and I wanted them so; and as I ran, they seemed to run too. I had such hard work to gather them; when at last I succeeded, my red cap dropped off; and without it I am as helpless as a mere mortal. While searching for the cap, which I have not found, a cock in the village crowed, and the fairies all fled away and left me. The door of the mound is closed, and for a whole long month there is no hope of my getting in again. Oh! I wish I could find my cap."

"If we help you to find the cap, will you stop crying?" said the children.

The shivering sprite wiped his eyes and promised that he would weep no more. The girl wrapped him in her apron, and then all three of them set out in search of the missing treasure. At last Timothy saw in the water around some reeds a red object which a bull-frog was opening his mouth to swallow; and, wading into the stream, he was able to rescue the magic cap, dry it in the sun, and restore it to its happy little owner.

"And now," said the smiling elf, who appeared to have suddenly grown old and wise, "as for a whole long month I am without a home, what do you say to taking me to yours? You will never regret it, that I promise you."

The children told their new friend what a poor place their home was, but the elf smiled and shook his head as if he knew what he was about. He bade the children lead him to their cottage, and once across the threshold of the wretched place, where the drunken mother was sleeping heavily on a pallet of straw in the loft above, the elf took his perch upon the mantel-shelf.

"Next, since I am obliged to live with mortals, let me see what the magic cap can do."

He put on the cap and immediately disappeared from the children's sight. When night came, Timothy fell asleep, but Bess watched; and at midnight she saw her new friend appear upon the hearth, conducting a perfect army of little workmen and workwomen. He waved his cap thrice around his head, and at once little carpenters set to building up the cottage-walls, little whitewashers made the ceilings wholesome, little painters covered all the woodwork with a coat of yellow. By sunrise what a change! The broken bricks of the floor were transformed into pretty blue and white tiles, lattice windows took the place of their old and dim ones, the pots and pans were scoured until they shone, roses looked in at the outer door, where rows of larkspur and of gillyflower, of bachelor's-button and "Love-in-a-mist" were growing on either side of a neat flagged walk to the garden gate. Instead of Timothy's old straw mattress, the boy lay on a clean white bed; and his sister, who had kept awake all night in utter wonderment, falling asleep at dawn, because her eyes refused to stay open any longer, found him shaking her arm, and begging her to come and share in the nice hot breakfast that—wonder of wonders!—their mother, sober, and clean, and smiling, had made ready at the fire.

It was a day of marvels! The mother seemed to have entirely forgotten her past degraded life, and was once more the brisk and rosy woman Simon had fallen in love with. A dozen times a day she paused in her spinning, or weaving, or baking, to run to the gate and wonder when dear father would come back. Timothy worked in the garden, Bess sewed and helped her mother, not daring to tell what she alone knew of the magic change. That night Bess slept, and Timothy kept watch. At midnight the fairy appeared upon the hearth, leading a dozen little bakers in white caps and aprons.

"Now make ready fifty loaves of your best white bread, that the goodwife may sell them on the morrow!" the fairy ordered; and at once the tiny men set to work mixing and kneading and baking, and at daybreak there were fifty of the sweetest white loaves money could buy. The fame of Simon's widow soon spread through the village, and every one was eager to see the wonderful reform worked in her, no less than in her cottage. Her bread was bought up as fast as she could furnish it, and next night Bess watched while Timothy slept. Then Bess saw the fairy appear at midnight, followed by a swarm of bees like a cloud.

"Make fifty pounds of your clearest honey, that the goodwife may sell it on the morrow."

The bees flew out of the door, and next morning the hives were found overflowing with luscious honey that smelt like a bed of clover all a-blow.

Next night came the bakers, and next night again the bees. Money flowed into the widow's purse as rapidly as it had once flowed out. Now was there lacking but one thing to complete their happiness, and that was the return of Simon to his family. Bess and Timothy together planned what they should do, and when the month had passed away, and the night of the full moon had come once more, neither went to bed, but both hid, watching for the coming of the sprite. Exactly at twelve o'clock, their kind little friend made his appearance, and summoning cooks and bees, ordered them to keep up their service on alternate nights, until the dame's coffers should be full to last a lifetime. Seeing him about to take leave, out rushed Timothy and Bess, threw themselves on their knees before the fairy, and, thanking him a thousand times over for his goodness, begged for one more act of grace—their father's release and restoration to his family. The fairy looked graver than they had ever seen him, and his brows puckered in a frown.

"Your father has committed an offence we never

pardon," he said, after a short silence. "He has been punished according to our laws, and must abide by the sentence, which is imprisonment for life."

The children burst into tears at this, and cried so that the fairy sneezed several times.

"I believe I am taking cold in all this dampness," he said, shivering slightly. "Come, dry up that deluge, and say good-by to me. The utmost I can do is to look up your father when I get back again, and tell him you are well and happy. I suppose you do not know that for some years past he has been attending our holiday frolics as musician, since our own best player broke his arm. Simon was under oath never to look at us, or to betray us, and this was the first time he transgressed. But our laws are very strict, and I am afraid to bid you even hope to see him again. One thing I may tell you. The king's chief counsellor has a mantle of red, worked with a device of six golden birds flying into a serpent's open jaws. If you should ever find that mantle, walk boldly to the oak-tree in the forest, knock three times, and cry, 'The King's Chief Counsellor!' Then you may be able to secure your father's freedom, but not else. And now, good-by to you."

THE FAIRIES AND THE FIDDLER.   125

The good elf vanished, and Timothy and Bess spent more time than ever in the forest. They had now taken their mother into the secret, for she, poor woman, had become as gentle and loving as she had before been hard and cruel. The one desire of the entire family was to get possession of the chief counsellor's mantle, but nothing seemed more unlikely.

A year passed, and Timothy had gone out to look at his rabbit-trap without particularly thinking of what it might contain, when a tremendous bustle inside attracted his attention. Cautiously he lifted the door, and up sprang an angry little man in green, having a long white beard, and a hump upon his back, who vanished from sight as quickly as he had appeared. Timothy lamented the loss of such unusual game, and then espied at the bottom of the trap nothing less than a tiny cloak of red, embroidered with six golden birds flying into a serpent's open jaws!

He made a joyful dive after the little garment, but, strange to say, it stuck tight to the fingers of his right hand, dragging after it the trap. Timothy shook it and pulled at it in vain; there it was, and not to be dislodged.

He ran home and called Bess to his assistance. The

little girl came out, and no sooner had she touched her brother than she stuck fast to him. The mother flew to the rescue, and became fastened to her daughter; and there they all were, in a long string, not knowing whether to laugh or cry at their strange predicament. The only thing was to make a pilgrimage to the oak-tree in the forest. Timothy's dog followed them, and rubbed against his master's coat. He, too, stuck fast, and so did Bessy's cat. Everybody they passed upon the way was attracted to the queer family party, and before long a little army of curious people were compelled to walk along in the direction of the forest.

Timothy did not know the secret of the little cloak, which had power to attract everything to it, drawing even people's thoughts out of their hearts, as a magnet draws the needle. Only in fairy-land could the objects so attracted be set free.

When they reached the oak-tree in the forest, Timothy struck upon it three times and called with a bold voice, though not without a trembling of the legs, for the king's chief counsellor. The bark of the great tree cleft slowly open, and out came the same old white-bearded fairy he had captured in the rabbit-trap. Bowing with mock humility, the old fellow asked what his visitors would be pleased to have.

"I demand my father, and also to be rid of this wretched little rag," said Timothy hotly.

"Step inside, step inside," said the elf with a malicious smile, for he knew that, once within, he might get the audacious mortals in his power, and force them to work his gold mines.

"Not a step will I go inside until I see my father," said Timothy firmly.

"Then here may you abide!" cried the old man, turning white with rage.

Timothy put one hand *within* the tree, holding the magic mantle at arm's-length.

"I demand my father," he cried in a loud voice.

The power of the mantle did not fail, for, rising from the darkness within, came poor blind Simon, stretching his arms toward his child, but holding tight his fiddle. At the moment Timothy's hand had come inside the fairy kingdom, the spell of enchantment was broken, and all of the strangely linked people were set free. Simon's wife and children threw their arms around him, and welcomed his return, while his neighbors shook his hand in warm congratulation. As for the old fairy, he fairly danced with rage. With the mantle in Timothy's possession, half the chief counsellor's power and reputation for wisdom would pass away. He offered rich bribes of gold and jewels, he threatened, he howled, he grinned, he hurled curses on their heads, but Timothy was firm.

"Then name your price, you wretch!" cried the angry fairy.

"It is that you shall restore my father's eye-sight," said Timothy.

This went very hard with the wicked old elf, who had been congratulating himself that Simon would bear away at least one mark of fairy vengeance. But he had met his match in Timothy, and there was no escape for the chief counsellor, who, diving down into the cavern beneath the hollow tree, reappeared fetching a box of magic ointment, which, rubbed upon Simon's eyes, made them better than ever.

When Simon saw not only the light of day, but his two dear children, and his wife looking as he had known her in her blooming youth, he uttered a cry of delight.

Then, to relieve his feelings, he struck up the old "Wind that Shakes the Barley," when, behold, not only all the people there assembled, but a score of little green folk, who had been in hiding, enjoying the discomfiture of the cross old counsellor, began to foot it on the greensward. Simon himself danced, and the old counsellor, sorely against his will, was forced to skip until his legs ached, for Timothy still held the mantle in his hand.

At last, when all were out of breath, the elf received his mantle. With a storm of angry words, he disappeared from sight. Immediately the sky darkened, a cold wind blew, and a shower of hail-stones fell upon our friends, sending them scampering and laughing away from the region where the fairy's spite prevailed.

Under the spell of the kind little sprite who had been their guest, the cottage was never approached by any unkind visitors. Simon fiddled and grew fat, his wife remained as sweet as fresh cream to the last day of her life, and their children came to be the pride of all the village.

So far as I have heard, that is the last visit Hayfield has had from the little men in green.

ETHELINDA; OR, THE ICE KING'S BRIDE.

ETHELINDA lived alone with her father, Count Constant, in a quiet country place, which had always been her home. Her mother was dead, and her father had long before fallen under the displeasure of his king, and was sentenced to exile for life in this lonely spot. Their castle was gray and venerable, half of it in ruins, and near by grew a grove of melancholy pine-trees; while only some stunted rose-bushes, and a black pool of water, in which swam a few antiquated carp, relieved the monotony of the grounds within the broken walls surrounding their dwelling.

One day a train of liveried servants on horseback, escorting a splendid carriage, stopped on the road near the castle.

Some accident had happened to the springs of the

vehicle, and the two passengers inside were forced to take refuge in the house of Ethelinda's father.

Count Constant himself, dressed in a faded court costume, but looking handsome and stately, came forth to receive his unexpected guests. He aided first a tall thin girl to descend from the broken carriage, and then, an elderly dame, richly dressed, who, throwing back her veil, revealed to him the face of his greatest enemy — the vindictive Duchess Amoretta. This person, whom he had not seen for years, had once been in love with Count Constant, and it was because he preferred to her the young lady who afterward became his wife, that the Duchess had poisoned the mind of his sovereign against him. To her he owed his banishment from court, and the loss of his estates. During his wife's lifetime he had heard nothing of the Duchess, and now to have to give her the shelter of his roof was a terrible ordeal.

The Duchess, however, was very kind and considerate in her manner to him. She made many apologies for the accident which had brought her there, and introduced to him her only child, the Lady Finella, who was, truth to tell, the most ill-tempered, pert minx ever seen, and a complete contrast to lovely Ethelinda.

During supper, which the poor Count's servants tried to make presentable with a few eggs cooked in

an omelette, a bottle of good wine, and a dish of stewed pigeons, the Duchess Amoretta was pleased with everything. She praised the cookery, she praised the tattered tapestries on the wall, she praised the Count's youthful looks, and she praised Ethelinda, till that modest maiden was quite overwhelmed.

When the two young ladies had retired (Ethelinda giving up her own little tower bedroom to her visitor, and creeping off somewhere to lie on a threadbare couch), the Duchess became confidential. She implored the Count to believe that enemies had come between them. She said that slanderers had arisen to tell him the wicked stories he had heard. She told him that her one desire was to see him restored to rank and fortune. And at last she drew from her pocket a paper signed by the King, in which the Count Constant was promised a free pardon on condition of his immediate marriage with the Duchess Amoretta.

The wily Duchess had planned the whole affair to get possession of her old lover again, and at first the Count, seeing himself caught in a trap as it were, was very angry.

Then the Duchess told him to think of his lovely young daughter, wasting her youth in this desolate spot. She promised to Ethelinda a life of happiness and prosperity. She worked upon the poor father with such artful words and lying promises, that, at last, Count Constant signed the contract, engaging to follow her in a few days to the capital, and there to give her his hand in marriage.

Ethelinda watched the fine chariot roll away with their unwelcome guests, next morning, and when it was out of sight, turned and threw herself upon her father's neck and kissed him fondly.

"How glad I am to get rid of them, papa!" she cried. "The daughter was so spoilt and haughty, and the mother was even worse; somehow I could only shudder when she kissed me, in spite of the beautiful bracelet she put upon my arm on taking leave."

"The Duchess means to be your best friend, my dear," her father said gravely, and went off to his study with a care-worn face. In a few days, he set out upon his journey to the capital, giving Ethelinda no idea of what he meant to do there.

Winter had set in, and a great snow fell. All the country-side was covered with a mantle of purest white. Ethelinda loved the frost and snow, and every day she put on her little brown hood and cloak with the scarlet lining, and set out for a walk in the forest, carrying a bagful of crumbs, which she would scatter for her favorite little birds. One day, while thus employed, she met an old woodman gathering sticks.

"Good-morning, daddy," said the girl in a pleasant tone.

"It's not a good morning with me, girl," the old man answered, crossly. "I'm frozen and starving too, thanks to this accursed snow."

"Don't speak ill of my dear snow," said Ethelinda, helping him to make his fagot. "Isn't it keeping the ground warm, and sheltering our roots and seeds for the spring-time? Come to the castle, if you will, and you shall have hot soup and a corner of the kitchen-fire. But you won't be allowed to abuse the beautiful work of the frost, in my hearing, that I'll promise you."

"Bravely said, fair maiden!" the old man exclaimed, dropping his bundle of sticks, and vanishing behind a screen of closely woven fir-trees. A moment later Ethelinda saw a sleigh containing a solitary traveller, drawn by a fleet black horse, dash by her like the wind. The sleigh was shaped like a silver swan and the bridle of the horse glittered with gems. The traveller appeared to be a tall and stately youth, with long fair locks and glowing cheeks. He was half hidden behind robes of snowy down, and as he shot swiftly by, leaving in his wake a breath of icy wind, Ethelinda fancied she heard him say, "We will meet again, dear lady, we will meet again!"

When, wondering over this incident, she reached the castle, it was to find there a letter from her father, commanding her immediate attendance at court, and announcing to her his marriage, which had already taken place.

Poor Ethelinda, full of astonishment, and fearing she knew not what, bade farewell to her dear home and journeyed to the castle of the Duchess Amoretta. Here she was received with tenderness by her father, who commended her in loving accents to the care of her new mother. Ethelinda could not help shuddering more than before when the dreadful, painted old Duchess stooped down to kiss her. She dared not look her father in the face, but it was easy to see that he was more unhappy in his new splendor than ever he had been in exile and in poverty. Ethelinda sighed deeply, and, looking around, encountered the snaky eyes of her new step-sister, fixed on her with wicked triumph.

And now, how changed was Ethelinda's life. Little by little, her father's companionship was withdrawn from her; his time was spent away from home, and soon, a war breaking out, Count Constant made haste to draw his sword in his king's service. A great battle ensued, and one of the first to fall, while gallantly fighting, was Ethelinda's father. He murmured a blessing on his child, and saying he was glad to go, died upon the battle-field, in the arms of his attendant.

The Duchess Amoretta, who by this time was heartily tired of having Ethelinda on her hands, now treated the poor girl with positive cruelty. A few months after the Count's death, she made up her mind to marry again, and in order to rid herself of her troublesome step-daughter, consulted with her own child, who was skilled in all sorts of wicked devices.

They built a summer-house extending over the river, and made in the floor of it a trap-door covered with moss and flowers, while beautiful vines grew around the pillars, and a fountain played in the centre. Into this pretty spot they invited Ethelinda to wander whenever she wished to be alone.

One day the poor girl went inside the summer-house, and began to weep for her father. Suddenly, a hand was extended by some one concealed behind the trellis-work of vines, and she was rudely pushed, so that she fell with all her weight upon the concealed trap-door, and instantly plunged into the rushing river below. One cry she uttered, and then to her astonishment, although it was the morning of a balmy summer's day, an icy breath blew over her, and above the surface of the river there arose a bridge of glittering ice, which she was enabled to cross in safety to the bank.

Making her way back to the house of her stepmother, Ethelinda was received with anger and astonishment. How she could have escaped, neither of her enemies could imagine. Ethelinda told nobody of the wonderful ice-bridge, which at the moment of her setting foot on shore had vanished like frost before the sun. A few days after, she desired to take her usual bath in the marble bath-room assigned to her use. No sooner had she entered the door than two strong women flew out from behind a curtain, and, seizing her by the shoulders, thrust her into a tank of boiling water they had prepared for the unfortunate girl.

Ethelinda saw that she was about to die a terrible death, and gave herself up for lost, when suddenly the icy wind she had twice felt before, blew over her. As the two furies plunged her into the tank, and rushed away, leaving her to her fate, she felt, instead of the scalding heat she expected, the delicious warmth of a tepid bath close round her limbs.

Again was she saved from evil by some unseen power; but now she knew what a terrible enemy was in pursuit of her, and determined to fly from the castle that very night. She hid in a little closet on the staircase, and, when night came, glided past the sleepy servants on guard, and escaped through the great gate into the open country.

Swift as her feet could carry her, Ethelinda fled. Out of the city, into the deep woods, under the cold glitter of the watching stars, the poor girl ran, every moment fancying that she heard the messengers of the cruel Duchess behind her. At last she fell down exhausted, saying to herself, "Better to die here from cold and starvation, than to be foully murdered by that wicked woman." She lay for a moment resting upon a bank of soft moss, and felt a sudden blast of icy wind.

Then was heard the cracking of a whip, and out of the woods came a sleigh driven by a solitary traveller.

Ethelinda had a vague idea that she had seen him

once before, but fainted away, and knew nothing more until she awoke to find herself in the sleigh, gliding swiftly along, wrapped in warmest robes of snowy fur.

"Save me, save me from the Duchess!" she murmured in a terrified voice.

"Sleep, poor child, you are safe now," a kind voice sounded in her ear. "Are you warm? Are you comfortable?"

"Very warm, very comfortable," Ethelinda answered, a strange drowsiness coming over her.

She slept again, and the black horse harnessed to the sleigh bounded forward like the wind. And now they passed through vast forests of pine and fir, into the regions of perpetual snow. For Ethelinda's guide was the young monarch of the frozen zone, and ruler of all ice and frost. Long had he loved the young girl secretly, and long had he vowed to make her his bride.

They stopped once, and now the sleigh was drawn by a span of magnificent reindeer, pure white, with collars of jewels, having their great antlers tipped with sparkling gems. Over snowy mountain peaks they glided, past chains of icebergs, with many a frozen sea shining far below like a sapphire. It was piercingly cold, and yet Ethelinda did not suffer. The only thing she could not control was her power of speech. Not a word could she utter, and the stranger, too, spoke no more, but smiled on her kindly, from time to time, as he drove ahead.

At last they reached a superb palace, built of ice, the roof fringed with icicles. An arch of many-colored lights spanned the roof, and from every door and window streamed forth a brilliant illumination.

"Welcome home!" said the stranger. "This is my palace, and you shall be my queen, fair maiden; for I am the King of the North Pole, and never, till now, have I seen one worthy to share my throne."

A train of milk-white bears with golden chains around their necks came out to receive the king and Ethelinda. They entered the palace, which blazed with splendid jewels on roof and walls. The throne was made of a single opal, and the queen's crown, which was immediately placed on Ethelinda's head, was composed of a circlet of diamonds, each one as large as a robin's egg.

The marriage took place at once; and Ethelinda's husband proved so kind and loving, that she soon forgot her early sorrows, and became as happy as all queens are supposed to be. Her fame spread into many countries; and after a time, some celebrated traveller, who visited her court, went back to the city where Ethelinda's wicked step-mother still lived and flourished, and gave the Duchess a message from the beautiful Queen of the North Pole.

"Tell her that I forgive her all her unkindness to me," Ethelinda had charged him to say, "since it was the means of securing to me my present joy, and the love of my dearest husband."

Ethelinda even sent gifts to her step-mother and sister; to each a jewelled necklace of immense value, and a robe woven from the down of the King's own eiderducks, which only sovereigns might wear. The Duchess and Finella eagerly seized the presents, but they almost died of spite to hear of Ethelinda's good luck. Night and day they wondered how they, too, might have similar fortune; and at length the Duchess determined to dress her daughter in coarse clothes like those Ethelinda had worn when found by the King of the North Pole, and to make her sally forth to the border of the forest.

Snow was falling fast when the young woman reached the wood. She was dreadfully cold, and began complaining and quarrelling, as usual. She did not hear the approach of a sleigh until it was close beside her. There sat a handsome youth, driving a fleet coal-black steed. He politely invited her to take a drive, and, with many groans over her stiff limbs, she got in. They flew over the ground, and for not a single minute did Finella cease finding fault with everything. She abused her mother for exposing her to this dreadful cold, and vowed she should have rheumatism and lumbago and pleurisy and influenza, all together, next day. Her feet had chilblains already, and her hands were so chapped they would never be fit to be seen. In this agreeable strain, she went on till her companion, growing impatient of her whining tones, blew a sudden breath upon her—when, behold! all the girl's conversation was frozen on her tongue, a few cross words, like icicles, clinging to the tip of it!

When they stopped at the palace door, the King of the North Pole (for he it was who had picked up Ethelinda's step-sister), instead of having her conducted in state to her apartments by a train of snow-white bears with golden chains about their necks, gave the cross girl in charge to an old brown bear of a housekeeper, with instructions to keep her locked up until the Queen should choose to set her free.

Ethelinda's kind heart softened toward her stepsister; and, begging the King to forgive her, the Queen hastened to set the prisoner at liberty. Finella, dressed in the Queen's own robes, was taken into the royal nurseries to see two splendid rosy babies, rolling upon soft furs, and romping with a gentle little bear-cub, who was their playmate.

The princes & their playmate.

When the step-sister saw these treasures, she conceived a wicked scheme of punishing Ethelinda through her love for them. So, pretending to repent of her past follies and unkindness, Finella was allowed by the King and Queen to live in comfort in their home.

On the night of some festivity (I believe it was a

special illumination by the Northern Lights), the King and Queen went off sleighing in style, through their dominions, leaving the babies in charge of their deceitful step-aunt, who always kissed them and caressed them, before folks, as though she loved them fondly.

As soon as the parents had disappeared, Finella ordered another sleigh to be harnessed, and taking the babies in her arms set forth. She attempted to guide the reindeer, but, in an instant, the great creatures were off like the wind, and soared up into the air, as the King himself had trained them to do. And now, how terrified was the wicked Finella! She knew no words with which to stop her fiery steeds, and presently sank, breathless and giddy, into the bottom of the sleigh. Higher, faster they went; the babies, like true sons of the frozen North, crowing with delight in the piercing atmosphere.

The sleigh stopped upon an iceberg, and there in the centre of the glittering blue pyramid sat the imprisoned older brother of the King of the North Pole. This wretch had been sentenced to be shut up there, because he had tried to kill his father, the late King. All of his body was changed to ice, excepting his heart, which burnt like fire. The reindeer Finella had taken were those accustomed to be driven by the King whenever he went to visit his wicked brother, whose eyes sparkled as he saw the little princes within his power. At last, he thought, he had a chance to be even with his enemies. He gnashed his teeth, shook his chains, and stretched out his long arms, inviting the travellers to come into his castle.

"I have golden apples and many pretty things for boys in here," he said deceitfully; but just as Finella, seeing her opportunity, was pushing the children out of the sleigh into the grasp of their cruel uncle, the reindeer set up a peculiar cry which could be heard half round the globe.

Instantly a chill wind blew, and riding on the wings

of a mighty sea-gull came the King of the North Pole. Fire flashed from his angry eyes, and his face was so terrible that the wicked sister and brother cowered and cringed before it. Snatching his babies in his arms, he replaced them unharmed in the sleigh. For a moment, he seemed about to crush both culprits to fragments in his wrath; but, relenting, he pronounced their sentence—and Finella was condemned to be the bride of the imprisoned brother. "Your fate is just," said the King of the North Pole, to the wretch within the iceberg; "I could not, if I tried, think of any worse punishment than to give you a complaining woman to share your exile."

And so Ethelinda was rid of her false step-sister, and from that day forth nothing occurred to disturb the serenity of the King's household.

As for the old Duchess (whose daughter had got a bridegroom she had not reckoned on in the northern country), she, like her hopeful child, lived and scolded forever and a day.

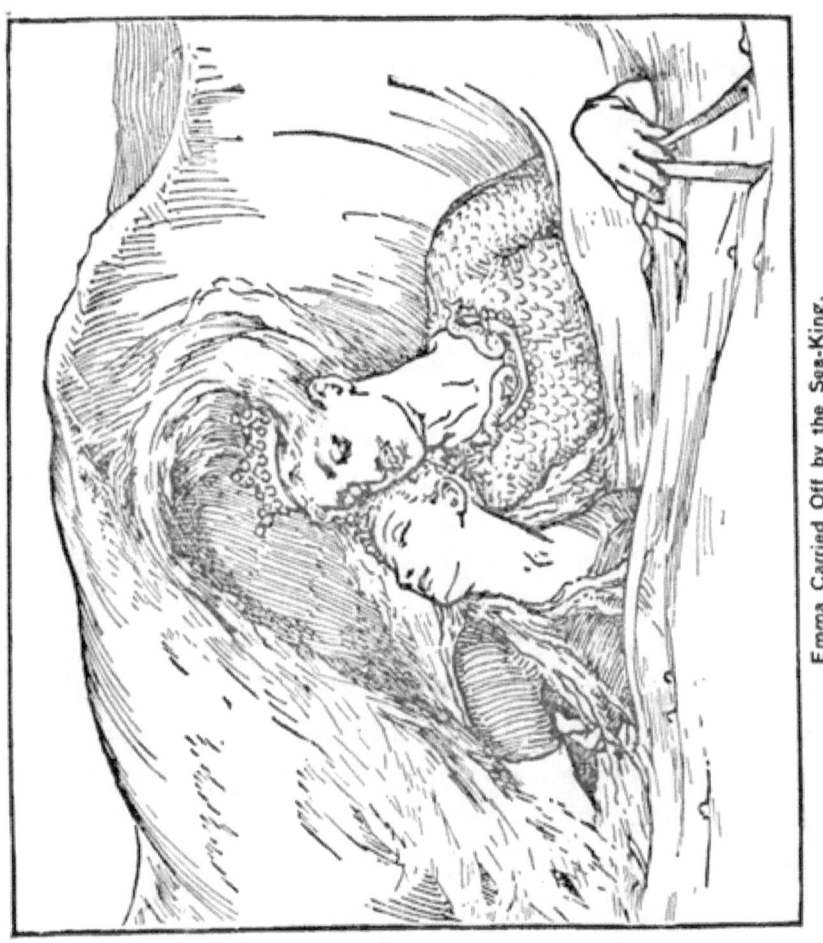

Emma Carried Off by the Sea-King.

DEEP-SEA VIOLETS.

IN a modest hut upon the sea-shore, half-hidden from sight by an enormous bank of drifted sand, lived a fisherman and his wife, with their twin-children, John and Emma. Theirs was a hard life, and full of privations; but the husband and wife loved each other tenderly and did everything they could to provide for the little ones, who grew up, spite of their poverty, tall and beautiful, and happy as the day was long. Emma and John had a thousand pleasures that town-bred children covet. They chased each other continually up and down the sandy beach, hard as marble and glittering like silver in the beautiful patterns traced on it by the tide. They ran barefoot into the surf, defying the mad onslaught of the merry breakers, and dived fearlessly beneath the crested arch of green waters to seize a bit of floating seaweed. They discovered endless treasures in the rock-pools along the beach, and built with them pretty grottoes, and mysterious caves, that none but themselves knew where to find. Often their father would take them out in the fishing-boat; for John had learned to manage the sail and the nets almost as well as the fisherman himself. The two children thought it was grand to feel the little boat answer to the wind, as a horse answers to voice or whip. They liked to bound forward across the great green billows, and to see the spray dash over them like a shower of jewels. They would help their father to set his nets or lines, and wait patiently till it was time to haul in the big shining fish that sometimes lined the bottom of the boat, whiling away the hours by munching bits of brown bread that served for lunch, and by telling each other fanciful stories of the sea.

The ocean did not always smile upon them, for there were days of heavy fog, of raw east wind, when the beautiful water ceased to sparkle, while the surf boomed as if in warning of danger or sorrow to come. Then the children would run inside the cottage, and pile on drift-wood till the fire burnt cheerily. This was their time for taking down from the mantel-shelf their stores of shells, corals, and other sea-wonders.

John and Emma had polished these shells until they shone beautifully, and some tiny disks of orange and gold were strung in long garlands, to loop around the brown walls and above the little looking-glass. Their mother kept the inside of the cottage as neat as a ship's cabin, which, in truth, it much resembled, the children's beds being nothing more than broad shelves in a cupboard, with doors to close by day; while every corner of the tidy place was made to do duty for some household implement, tucked away in the oddest fashion, until it should be needed.

So the days passed on until the twins were about sixteen years old, John a fine manly fellow, looking much older, and Emma a slender slip of a girl, with floating locks of purest gold, and a voice in singing like a carol of birds in a Maybush. Oftentimes when her father was steering his boat homeward, after a day of toil, he would hear the piercing strain of Emma's song come floating over the water from the rock where she stood against the western sky, awaiting him. And he rightly thought this the sweetest sound he was likely to hear before the angels should sing for him in Paradise!

One day the fisherman did not come home. A storm arose, and all that evening the wind howled madly

Emma Singing on the Rocks.

above the beating of the angry surf. The sky was pitch-black, and the wife and children walked the shore in silent fear. When darkness fell, they lighted a huge bonfire upon the rocks, and John, begging his mother and Emma to go home to rest, stayed feeding the flames with drift-wood, till morning broke over the sullen waste of waters. Still no sign of his father, and at midday the familiar boat drifted ashore, bottom upward. Then great sorrow darkened this happy little home; and nevermore the sea gave up her dead.

The fisherman's wife did not long survive him—dying, she told her children, because she could not live without her beloved husband. John followed his father's calling, and Emma kept the house, as her mother had done. She was very sad and solitary in the changed life, but people who work hard have not much time to give way to grief. The busy maiden toiled all day over her duties in-doors, and when evening came, would go out on the rocks to await John's return. The greatest pleasure she now had was in singing. Her voice grew strong and firm, and every day at sunset it might be heard, in waves of melody, mingling with the sound of the breakers on the shore.

One day, when John was later than usual in returning to his supper, Emma wandered along the sands. It was a beautiful summer evening, the sky painted with radiant colors, the sea reflecting them. Here and there a sail dotted the horizon, but the shore was completely deserted. The girl saw before her a rock-pool filled with sea-anemones and star-fish; and, sitting down on the edge of it to study the lovely creatures, she began, as usual, to sing, without knowing that she did so.

Suddenly, over the water came rolling toward her a wonderful chariot formed of a single conch-shell all rainbow-hued within. It was drawn by two dolphins, and the driver was a handsome young man, whose long floating locks were of a changeable green color, tipped with curling white. Before Emma could recover from her astonishment, the youth spoke to her gently, thanking her for the song that had wooed him from his home beneath the sea.

"I am the king of a wonderful country down there," he said, "and if you will but sing for me once more, I shall give you gems and flowers from my own garden, such as never an earth-born maiden owned."

Dipping one hand carelessly over the chariot's edge, the king brought up a string of rare carved coral with a jewelled clasp, and, smiling at Emma's wonder, dipped his hand a second time, when out came a garland of exquisite flowers. Sea-lilies, sea-roses, sea-narcissus, sea-violets there were, larger and more beautiful than any upon land, and all glittering with the ocean brine. Emma stretched out both hands for the pretty things, while a song of joy burst from her lips.

"May I crown your brow with my garland?" said the king. "For truly, I have heard no voice to equal yours."

"Thanks—thanks," cried the innocent girl, her eyes sparkling with delight. She leant forward to receive the chain which the king threw around her neck, at the same time laying the garland on her hair. At once, Emma fell into a deep sleep, and the crafty sea-king, with a look of triumph, lifted her into the seat at his side and urged forward his chafing steeds; the chariot flew like a stormy petrel across the sea, disappearing beneath the arch of a gigantic wave!

John sought in vain for his cherished sister. The only trace of her, he and the neighbors who helped him in the search, could find, was a little gold cross, once her mother's, that Emma always wore. This lay in a crevice of the rock, whence the sea-king had carried her away. The neighbors believed her dead, but something within John convinced him that he should see her yet again. Long and dreary were the winter months without her. John forever wondered about Emma's disappearance; and, when summer came once more, it was to find the youth still possessed of a longing desire to go somewhere in search of her.

Sad and solitary, John was sailing his little fishing-smack along the coast one day, intending to go out to the usual fishing-ground, when, tempted by a creek he noticed now, as if for the first time, a fancy took him to follow up the windings of this silver inlet from the sea, running between banks as green as emerald. Looking into the water, as a light breeze carried him along, John saw a bed of weed and kelp starred with shells, where crabs of an unusual size passed in and out of a circular opening. Determined to fill a basket with these desirable dainties, which would fetch a high price in market, John fished for them so skilfully as to haul up a hand-net brimful, at the first attempt. These were no common crabs he discovered, one of them in particular, having its flippers set with rings of beaten gold, and a gold chain around its body bearing a golden key.

"My good sir," said the crab, speaking in a plaintive voice, "you probably don't know that I am the keeper of the sea-king's summer grotto, and these are my attendants. Only to-day, his majesty sent us word to have all in readiness for a visit from him and his bride-betrothed. We are in the greatest possible hurry, and if it is quite the same to you, would take it as a friendly favor, if you will let us go without delay."

"My good Mr. Crab," said John, laughing, "I should like to oblige such an important person, but really my circumstances are almost as particular as yours. I am in the greatest possible need of funds, and the price you and your friends would fetch at the present market rates is most desirable to me."

"Oh! if it is only gold and silver," said the crab, disdainfully, "you should see his majesty's dominions. Our streets are paved with it."

John became interested at this, and entered into a long conversation with the crab, who was a gossipy old soul and told him of so many wonders of the sea-king's kingdom that the lad could scarcely contain his astonishment.

What startled him more than all, was to hear of a sweet singing maiden, from the upper world, his majesty had kept for a year past imprisoned in a crystal cavern! His heart beat fast with excitement, as the crab described Emma so exactly that it was impossible to mistake her.

"Until the present time," the crab went on, with importance, "his majesty has not told the earth-maiden of his intention to make her his bride. By the laws of our kingdom, no one of us can marry a mortal, until she has lived for a year contentedly below, without uttering the name of any friend she knew in her former estate. But the year is up to-day, and they are to make a grand tour of his majesty's possessions. I should not wonder if the wedding were to take place in our grotto, for that is the king's favorite palace, although only one of the many he calls his own."

"One thing is false! Emma will never marry him, if she is to do it by forgetting those who loved her so tenderly," broke in John, furiously.

"You are very rough, my dear friend," said the crab, fanning himself with his flipper. "I think you forget you are addressing a courtier. What I tell you about the Lady Emma is undoubtedly true, since I have it from my cousin the clam. He is a close-mouthed creature, little likely to spread a false report.

Lady Emma is happy as a queen in swansdown. Once a day she sings, and then his majesty always presents her with a bunch of fresh sea-violets, her favorite flowers. Under the circumstances, it is hardly possible she would keep up any of the foolish fancies for earth-born folk she may have brought there."

John pondered awhile, and finally promised the crab, who was growing very impatient, to release that functionary and his companions, if they would permit him to visit the wonders of the sea-king's grotto. The crab, since he could not well help himself, said yes, and instructed John how to dive into the round green hole, so like the nest of some strange fish, he saw at the bottom of the stream.

John made fast his boat, and sprang overboard, having first emptied the net full of captives, who went scuttling to the bottom in very undignified haste. So sure was his aim, that he reached without difficulty the passage-way indicated, which widened from its mouth into a funnel-shaped cavern, lined with seaweed and ferns of the rarest varieties. Following the crab procession, John swam along a crystal streamlet, reaching at length a second opening, larger than the first. Within this was a door formed of a single sapphire. The crab put his golden key into the key-hole, and admitted John into a large and brilliant grotto, the sides lined with the iridescent scales of fish. The roof was encrusted with jewels, through which streamed many colored lights, and clusters of phosphorescent flame gleamed at intervals between pillars of glittering spar. Beneath an arch of blooming sea-flowers, stood

a throne made of snowy coral branches, and cushioned with velvet moss. At its foot was a pillow of blue violets, another one hanging at the back. A tiny stream of clear water ran down the cavern's side, and shot up in a fountain in the centre. John's eyes blinked with pleasure when he came into the pretty place, but the sound of approaching music made the crab hurry him into hiding, with the order on no account to risk showing himself in the presence of the king, who would instantly have him hugged to death by a giant devil-fish. John kept quiet, you may be sure. The crabs formed into double rows, bowing and scraping, in token of their deep reverence for the king (they had been selected to be courtiers in consequence of their facility in walking backward), and the sight almost made John laugh aloud; but he was soon reduced to silence, not only by the imposing entry of the monarch of the seas, but because, in the bride-betrothed, he saw indeed his own dear Emma.

Emma was greatly changed in appearance. She now wore a splendid robe of some clinging white stuff, worked with little coral branches and sprays of seaweed around the hem, and her neck, arms, and hair were wreathed with row upon row of priceless pearls. She was pale, but more beautiful than ever, and on her breast John saw a knot of big blue violets. Emma was seated at the king's right hand, and lovely sea-nymphs danced before her, to the music of unseen orchestras. Then his majesty asked Emma to sing, pledging her health in a shell full of wine, that shone and sparkled beautifully. Emma made no resistance, doing all that she was bid, like a person walking in her sleep. Her eyes had a far-away look and her voice, in singing, so unearthly a thrill, that John's affectionate heart ached to seize her in his arms and tear her from the spot. When Emma had finished singing, she appeared to be fatigued, and two sea-nymphs bore her to a couch of pearl, laid her on purple cushions, and combed her long hair with a golden comb, while other sea-maidens interlaced their white arms above the girl's head, soothing her to sleep.

"Let her sleep here till this day week," said his majesty. "Then I will summon my subjects and relations to the wedding. All of you present withdraw, now, and on no account disturb her slumber."

When the coast was clear, John seized his opportunity, and stealing forth, knelt beside his sleeping sister, and whispered in her ear. Emma moved, her eyes opened slowly, and uttering a deep sigh, she looked her brother full in the face. But alas! she did not recognize him. In despair, John seized her hand, and tried to urge her to fly with him. He reminded her of her home, of their happy childhood, of their dead parents, of everything that could touch the heart. All in vain! Emma smiled sweetly, and stroked his head as, shedding bitter tears of disappointment, he bent it upon her knees; but she knew him not.

"Leave me in peace," she said, "I am the sea-king's bride-betrothed, and you are but a poor fisher's lad. What you say to me of earth and home I do not understand. This is my home, and if the king should find you here, he would take your head off. If you love me as you say, please go."

Emma lifted to her face the cluster of purple violets, and at once her lids drooped; and, sinking back upon her purple cushions, she slept again.

In bitter disappointment, John retraced his way along the vestibule of the king's grotto and emerged into the inlet where his boat was moored. Carefully marking the spot, he returned to it the next night, but no trace could he find of the submarine opening. The old crab had taken good care to prevent another visit from a marauder, who might cost him his life. John felt ready to abandon all hopes, when, leaning over the edge of the boat, and dragging the water through habit, he felt a violent struggling and fluttering within the net. Hauling it quickly in, a swarm of silver-bright little fishes, each one wearing a pretty maiden's head, escaped from the meshes, leaving behind but a single token, and that John found to be a tiny golden harp. He drew his fingers across the strings, and the sweet sound it gave out was echoed by a sob from beneath a rock ledge close at hand.

"Who is there?" cried John.

"It is I—chief of the sea-king's minstrels," said a

voice. "This evening, I and my band were amusing ourselves by the light of the moon, when your cruel net almost frightened us to death. Oh! what shall I do? It's nearly time for the king's visit to his bride-

betrothed in the grotto; and if you will not restore to me my harp, I shall be behind-hand, and in disgrace. Oh! if you only knew how strict the leader of the court orchestra is!"

"Will you take me into the grotto, if I give the harp to you?" said John, firmly.

"Oh! I dare not," cried the little mermaid, shivering. "Only yesterday, his majesty found out that some rude outsider had found his way into the grotto, and he has placed on either side of the entrance a double-headed shark. For you to attempt to pass them would be certain death! Pray, pray ask something easier; for every moment is precious to me, now."

"Then tell me what has caused Emma to forget all her life on earth?"

"That I can do, right easily," said the mermaid, coquettishly; "for I have a sister in the band of especial hand-maidens set apart by the king to wait on the bride-betrothed. The fresh violets sent every day to Lady Emma by his majesty, have the power to make her forgetful, and indifferent to all save her present surroundings."

"I knew she had not really grown cold," cried John, in a burst of gratitude. "Here is your harp, pretty one, but answer me one question more. How can I find the entrance to the grotto?"

The little mermaid stood on tip-tail to receive her harp, and, as she once more clasped it in her arms, whispered, in a frightened tone: "When the moon is at the full, its rays strike a white cliff over against yonder dark coast-line. Steer your boat evenly along the path traced by those rays upon the water, and you may see the wedding procession go in at the state entrance. But, of all things, take care not to let yourself be perceived, for on this occasion all the monsters of the deep will be on guard, and your life would not be worth a broken clam-shell."

John bade the mermaid good-by, and from that moment all his thoughts turned upon how he might obtain admission to the wedding festival. He cast his nets diligently, but with no success. All the fishes seemed to have deserted their usual haunts; and no wonder, for the entire population of the sea was in a state of preparation for the great event.

At last the night of the full moon came, and you may be sure John was abroad and watchful, as he cast his nets in feverish anxiety. A sudden pull made him haul in rapidly, and this time he was rewarded by a catch that cost him the most tremendous struggle. What was his surprise to drag into the boat a huge fish, six feet long, with a tall fin nearly the length of its body. The most curious part of it was that the tips of this fin, and also a patch on the creature's head, shone with imprisoned fire. Along the sides of the body were a double row of luminous spots. The fish made no further fight, and John gazed at him in admiration.

"In the name of wonder, what have we here?" he said.

"My good sir," answered the fiery fish, "if you had the least idea of the nature of my business, I am sure you would not interrupt me for a moment. I am one of his majesty's torch-bearers, and the procession is already forming to go to the grotto of the bride-betrothed."

"Hurrah!" said John. "If you will manage to take me with you, I will let you go, but not else."

In vain the torch-bearer protested and begged. John was inexorable. In the end, the torch-bearer demanded time for reflection, and at last spoke as follows:

"I and four of my brothers lead the way, and by going with me you would certainly be seen and punished. But at the very tail-end of the procession, my old father and mother will jog along, accompanied by a swarm of their younger grandchildren. These pretty little creatures, as you may not know, are called Bombay ducks, and their whole bodies glow with light. They are very good-natured, and if we can but win over the other family who help to light the court festivals, the Chiasmodos, I believe we might smuggle you in unobserved between the old people."

"Who are the Chiasmodos?" asked John.

"They are a tribe of deep-sea light-givers," said the torch-bearer, "who consist entirely of a mouth and a stomach. The latter organ swells to an enormous size, and floats beneath like a transparent balloon, while above their great, wide-grinning mouth is worn a crown of light. They are rather snappishly inclined, these Chiasmodos, and may give us trouble; but we must run the risk, if you insist. So, come along, young man, there's no time to waste in talking."

John did not hesitate, but overboard he went, swimming after the released torch-bearer, who proved a friendly fellow after all. It was a beautiful summer's night, and the moon shed a path of radiant light upon the ocean, lying calm and serene beneath her spell. John and the torch-bearer swam along a track of liquid silver, and opposite the white cliff they saw a marvellous array.

The procession was formed, and about to take up its line of march. The drum-fishes were already beating a roll-call; the fiddler crabs fiddled wildly; while the sea-lions roared and rumbled, the whales blew their trumpets, the porpoise puffed, and the electric eel, who was the court jester, wriggled along the line, playing foolish tricks and giving unexpected shocks to those who did not pay attention. Such a multitude! To describe them all would fill many pages of this book; and besides, you would never be able to remember the hard names. The pilot-fish cruised around in front, the torch-bearers came next, then the mermaid musicians, and a host of sea politicians with banners, preceding the whales who sailed majestically ahead of the king's chariot of pearl, drawn by twelve milk-white dolphins with jewelled harness.

After them, every conceivable kind of fish, in regular order, according to their dignity. The octopus party was a sight to make one shudder, but they were in a good humor for once, and comparatively beaming. The sea-serpent swam alone, considering himself too much of a rarity to associate with every-day folk. The sword-fish saluted, and the skates tried to smile, but only succeeded in looking more hideous than before, very much as if they had pains under their waistcoats. The brilliant angel-fishes and the fairy nautilus made the most lovely show it is possible to imagine ; though it is hardly fair to single out one or two for praise, when all did so well. Even the herrings from the public schools, and the vulgar little porgies, had clean faces and were allowed to tag after the procession. And, last of all, came the cross Chiasmodos, fortunately swimming before the old father and mother torch-bearers, who, between them, carried John along, and were followed by a gleaming myriad of little Bombay ducks, true glow-worms of the sea.

Led by the moon rays to the white cliff on the coast, the procession came to a halt; and immediately a pair of hidden doors flew back and revealed a long tunnel glittering with lights, which opened directly into John's well-remembered grotto.

There, within, stood Emma, decked in bridal lace, worked by ancient mermaids thousands of years before, to be worn by the queen at her bridal ; and on her head was a fragrant crown of violets. She smiled as the king approached, and gave him her hand ; the wedding at once began. John, hidden behind a projecting crag, saw, with despair in his heart, the ceremony go on.

The entire walls were lined with ranks of octopi and sharks on guard. To defy them would be death to Emma and himself. He leaned further forward than he intended, and was seen by one of the Chiasmodos, who, flashing her lantern in his face, at once informed on him to her neighbor. Immediately a new monster swam toward John. This was another of the deep-sea torch-bearers, the Chanliodus, appointed to act as chief sentry to the cave. A more ferocious countenance cannot be imagined than was his. The wide mouth bristled with sharp fangs, and his fins were tipped with flame, while all along his sides extended a row of spots like little windows in a ship, through which light was shining.

John saw that in another moment he would be lost. So long as the bridal procession was going on, no one dared to speak ; and, beckoning the fierce creature to come behind the rock, John met it with an open knife, aiming so skilfully as to cut the fish open its entire length. The idea now occurred to him to place himself within the body of his dead enemy, which he promptly did, and to his joy, could swim out unobserved, and take his place at the bride's right hand. Just as Emma was about to say " I will," the sentry-fish managed to place in her hand the little gold cross that was once her mother's. The queen-elect looked at the cross in surprise, and as all had passed so quickly, not even the king understood why her head drooped forward, and she seemed about to faint. The sentry-fish whispered in her ear:

"It is I—John—your brother; be brave, and find some excuse for putting off the wedding, and we may yet be saved."

So long as Emma wore the crown of violets, she was unable entirely to break the charm they cast over her. But the little cross was a powerful reminder of her life on earth; and while she held it, she appeared to be awakening from a trance. Excusing herself to the king on the ground of illness, she was supported to her coral couch, and was surrounded by her mermaidens. The king ordered the crowd to withdraw, and soon the disappointed revellers went away, feeling blue and cross, while his majesty himself was in a terrible way, tramping up and down, tearing his green locks, and casting himself on his knees beside Emma, imploring her to speak to him once more.

In vain! Emma's eyes were now obstinately closed, and her cheeks were like marble. The faithful sentry-fish, whose duty it was to patrol the grotto, swam up and down before the couch, and every time he passed near Emma he whispered, "Be brave. I am here. Soon I will rescue you. Give no sign of life."

At last the king took the advice of an old dowager mermaid, and left Emma to herself, consenting to go outside the grotto and smoke a seaweed cigarette, until his bride should be ready to go on with the interrupted wedding.

John spied in the train of mermaidens the little creature whose harp he had restored, and very cautiously, for fear of alarming her, he made himself known. The pretty mermaid laughed and cried hysterically, when she heard his story, and consented to aid him still further by removing the crown of violets from Emma's head. Soon there was heard a great whispering among the mermaid band, and one of the boldest of them ventured to suggest to the dowager lady-in-waiting, that one reason for her majesty's continued swoon might be that her hair was plaited too tight. The dowager, for a wonder, took the suggestion in good part. She ordered the attendants to unpin her majesty's long golden braids, and in so doing the fatal crown fell to the ground unnoticed.

The blood rushed into Emma's face; she sighed, and opening her eyes, looked about her. There was the band of anxious mermaids, and a solitary sentry-fish swimming up and down. In next passing her, he whispered, "Order your attendants to withdraw." This was soon done, only the friendly little mermaid remaining at Emma's side. John, throwing off his disguise, clasped his sister in his arms, and warm tears of human happiness rushed from Emma's eyes. Trampling under foot the crown of violets, and keeping firm hold of her mother's cross, she begged John to bear her back to their own world without delay. Cautiously putting on his fish garb, John swam to the door to reconnoitre the situation. He found there, on guard, only one of the shark sentries, who had taken so much sea-beer, in honor of the king's wedding-day, that John's knife made quick work in despatching him.

And now the way seemed open for their flight. The brother and sister bade farewell to the friendly mermaid, who pledged herself never to reveal the secret of Emma's escape, and started to leave the grotto. Suddenly, lashing the sea in his wrath and fury, both of his fierce mouths spiked with rows of terrible teeth, came the other double-headed shark! John still wore his

Chanliodus disguise, and, without a moment's hesitation, dashed bravely to meet the foe. Wielding his trusty knife, he stabbed the shark again and again through the body, darting aside before the monster could get the advantage of him. The shark, wounded mortally and mad with rage, darted forward in a final effort, but John planted his knife in its open jaws. Uttering a horrid death-shriek, the creature lay without motion upon the threshold of the cave.

John lost no time, for the noise of the conflict had already attracted to the scene a number of curious loungers; and, as he feared, the king himself, attended by his body-guard of monsters, now came in sight. Darting swiftly through the waves, with Emma clinging bravely to his shoulders, the assumed Chanliodus drove his sharp fin abruptly into the middle of a party of squids. These poor fellows were the disappointed reporters of a submarine newspaper, going home *without* an account of the wedding for their journals! The suddenness of the attack caused the squids promptly to spill the contents of the ink-pots they always carry with them, forming a dense black cloud, under cover of which the fugitives safely reached the surface of the sea.

The sun was rising, its rosy light lying upon the

bright ocean like a veil. Now, they knew they were secure, for so long as the sun rules in heaven, the sea-king dares not show himself above the waves. John and Emma gazed upon the shore, finding themselves but a little distance from their boat at anchor, and wept tears of joy and thanksgiving for their deliverance from the horrors of the deep. When they had clambered into the boat, John begged his sister to cast away the embroideries and the ropes of pearl she had brought from the sea-king's dominion. Even as he spoke, they saw Emma's finery vanishing like a wisp of burnt paper, while her lovely pearls had turned into strings of common pebbles. Of all her ornaments only the little golden cross remained, and that shone with new lustre. With the full force of his stalwart arm, John cast the sea-king's tokens far into the water; and as they sank, both brother and sister fancied they saw a huge hand arise to seize them with an angry grasp, and heard a growl of baffled rage beneath the waves. Wrapping his sister in his fisherman's cloak, John hastened to sail back to the humble hut beneath the sand-drift, which had never looked so lovely in their eyes.

There they dwelt, loving and serene, until in due

time a good husband came for Emma, and John took to himself a fair young wife. From that day forth, prosperity attended them, and John sailed his own ships across the ocean, while Emma lived in a beautiful home near the shore. Strangely enough, never again did John succeed in entrapping one of the talking creatures of which, as we have clearly seen, there are plenty in the sea, if one has luck to find them! And another curious thing is, that never again was Emma able to lift her voice in song. The beautiful gift which had brought about her strange adventure, and had well-nigh proved so fatal to them both, had been lost forever!

THE WILD WOODSMAN DISGUISED AS A TRAVELLER.

THE WILD WOODSMAN.

ONCE there lived a peasant whose only daughter, Martha, had eyes as blue as corn-flowers and long hair like the silk around an ear of corn. All the lads of the village were after her, but she cared only for John, a young huntsman, who was called by her father an idle vagabond, and sent away from his cottage in disdain. Now, the village where they lived was at the foot of a high mountain covered with a dense forest, into certain portions of which few were found to venture, so wild and lonely they were. One day Martha went, unknown to her father and mother, to ramble in the forest. She said to some of her friends that she meant to gather flowers and pick berries, to sell to a rich lady who lived near them; but the truth was, that a week had passed without John having set foot in the village, and she was anxious and uneasy, and wished to visit some of her lover's favorite haunts, to see if he might be there. It was no uncommon thing for John to be absent for several days, while trapping and hunting. He could sleep as well on a bank of moss as on his pallet at home, and he loved to go to rest under the broad canopy of the sky, studded with bright stars, and to be lulled by the music of falling waters.

Martha, dressed in her brown cotton frock, with the scarlet handkerchief knotted over her fair hair, was seen to go up a rocky pathway on the mountain-side, where the firs and larches made a bower overhead; but that night she did not come home, and next day, when John came into the village with a splendid string of birds he had shot miles away from there, in an opposite direction to the one Martha had taken, it was to hear the sad news of the poor girl's disappearance.

John's face grew pale and his stout heart grew faint; he thought of what all the others were thinking of—the Wild Woodsman, against whose magic his gun and staff might avail nothing!

The mountain above was believed to be the haunt of a mysterious being, half man, half brute, fierce and cruel, from whose den no living creature might ever be rescued. The Wild Woodsman, for so the natives called him, took many a shape to trap unwary travellers, and a fair young girl like Martha would be a rich prize for him. John had long vowed to capture the Wild Woodsman; and now he was filled with a mad thirst to seek him at once. Without stopping to hear more, the young man rushed off up the steep mountain path, bounding like a chamois from rock to rock, as the villagers, awe-struck and tearful, gazed after him and crossed themselves in superstitious fear.

Through brake and brier, John darted on; he was soon in the dark recesses of the forest, where the undergrowth was like a jungle. His fleet foot never tired in the chase, and, erelong, he spied a little red handkerchief upon the ground. Recognizing this to be Martha's, he gazed about him, and saw, by the token of broken bushes, that the girl had been dragged away from that spot up a rocky wall, which it seemed to him no foot could scale.

Struggling to keep down his sickening dread, John determined to follow. He began to climb the steep rock. His faithful dog, who had kept close beside him, suddenly gave a low fierce growl, and the hair on its back bristled up in fury. John was already half-way up the cliff, when, on looking down, there, just where he had picked up the handkerchief, he saw a queer little old fellow, making shoes as quietly as if nothing at all had happened.

"Hallo, there!" roared John, for he suspected mischief.

The old man looked up, and John saw that he had a young and rosy face with hair as gray as a badger's. The odd creature made signs that he was stone deaf, and beckoned John to come down. All this time, the dog was growling fearfully, and John took warning from the sign. He levelled his gun without more ado, and said:

"Answer, you fellow. Who are you that have cheeks so fair, and an old man's locks?"

"I?" said the old man, hopping up with a dreadful grin, "you will know me soon enough, sirrah, for I am the devil's grandfather."

He stretched out an arm that grew longer every minute, and his hands changed to the claws of a beast. John lost no time, but taking aim fired at the Wild Woodsman, for he it was, and none other. Bang! The friendly bullet made straight for the creature's heart, and though it did not kill him outright, the Wild Woodsman was sorely wounded. He fell over a log, groaning pitifully, and prayed John to come to the aid of a poor old man. John said, "That I will with another bullet," when the Wild Woodsman darted from the spot, and was lost in the thicket.

After him went the dog, after the dog went John. Such a hunt there never was! Through spots in the woods where man's foot had never penetrated, into bogs, and into serpents' lairs, past the caves where bears were lurking; but no animal would touch John, for the Wild Woodsman was their deadly enemy.

At last they came to a cleft in a little green hillock. Here was a hut covered with moss, and the Wild Woodsman, uttering a frantic yell, fell dead upon the threshold. John heard a shriek within the hut, and, dashing down the door, saw Martha, lying, bound with ropes made of plaited willow, in a corner.

He flew to set her free; but, to his surprise, Martha did not appear to know him. She let him take her by the hand and lead her from the fearful spot where the inner walls were built of the bones of the Wild Woodsman's victims. She looked up into his face and smiled, and John saw she had lost her reason. He did not stop to pick up the jewels and gold, stolen from murdered travellers, with which the hut was strewn, but made all speed to leave behind the horrid place. He lifted Martha in his strong arms and carried her down a path along the far side of the mountain. A great storm arose, and the earth trembled under his feet; but he kept bravely on his way, and looking back saw the cleft in the hills widen; then a great gulf opened, fire and smoke burst forth, and the hut of the Wild Woodsman was swallowed forever from sight.

John gave a shout of joy, and began singing a hymn in his clear young voice. The storm ceased. The clouds parted. Down in the valley below was their own peaceful village, and the sound of the evening bells came floating up to him. Martha, who had lain in his arms as if asleep, stirred, and recognized him. Her strength returned, and she asked to walk beside him. Strangely enough, she said nothing of her late adventure, then or ever afterward. Not a trace of it remained in her memory.

When they reached the village, all the people came out to meet them, rejoicing. John told them he had rescued the lost girl, but the true history of his chase of the Wild Woodsman he kept to himself. Martha's father and mother greeted her with tears of thankfulness; and before another year had gone by John and Martha were married in the village church. From that day forth, peace reigned upon the mountain-side; but when stories of the Wild Woodsman were told to Martha's grandchildren, they little knew the share their hale old grandsire had in ridding the country-side of such a scourge.

THE FROZEN HEARTH-FAIRY.

ONCE upon a time, there were a poor couple who lived in a little cottage overgrown with vines. From roof-tree to cellar, their home was as clean as hands could make it, and the table and chairs were scoured every day till they were as white as snow. The man went out into the woods to tie up fagots, and the woman kept a few bees, and sold the honey. In this way they managed to live, and were happy, till a great storm came, and swept off the roof of their house; then the lightning set it on fire, and it was soon burned to the ground. The man came running from the forest, and found his wife crying as if her heart would break, beside her bee-hives, which the wind had upset, scattering all their busy inmates, and destroying the honey.

"Where shall we sleep to-night?" said the wife.

"Let us search till we find," answered the husband. So they set off and wandered into the woods, while the storm raged over them. Long did they stray, until night came. At last they saw a ruined hut, left by some charcoal-burners, and thankfully entered it. There was dry straw in one corner, and here the poor woman laid down, half dead with fright and fatigue. Both of them were hungry, and the man putting his hand in his pouch was glad to find there a bit of bread, which he was about to give to his wife, when a queer little black object sprang down the wall and seized the crust, running nimbly off with it.

"Who are you?" cried the poor man.

"I'm a lost hearth-fairy," said the little creature, in a piping voice. "If you had made me a fire to warm my poor bones, I should not have taken your food."

The hearth-fairy's teeth were chattering, and the man pulled together some sticks and straw, and lighted them with his flint and steel. The smoke curled up, the flames sparkled merrily. The hearth-fairy slid down and warmed himself.

"Hallo there! give me back my crust," said the poor man, whose wife kept pulling him by the sleeve, to remind him of her hunger.

"Now that I think of it, I want this crust myself," said the hearth-fairy. "I am off on a journey to seek a warm fireside, and I need something to strengthen me. But here is a duck instead, only you had better not kill her!"

A fine fat duck tumbled at the poor man's feet. The hearth-fairy vanished in the smoke. Oh! how the poor couple longed to kill and eat that duck. Their mouths watered as they thought of onion-sauce, and of bread-crumbs, and of sage. Faint and starving, they fell asleep in a corner of the hut. When day broke the poor man rose up, and went to the door. The storm had ceased and the duck was quacking on the door sill. She waddled away, and left behind her a large egg of purest gold. Just then the lord of the forest rode by with his huntsman.

They saw the shining prize in the poor man's hand, and offered to buy it of him.

"I will give it for a loaf of brown bread and a sausage," he said, "for my wife lies starving, within."

The huntsman gave him food and drink; and the lord of the forest, after hearing his story, had the poor couple taken to a nice empty cottage near by, and told them they should have it for their own. The golden egg was sold, and the man and his wife lived in comfort all their days from the money it fetched. They never saw either the hearth-fairy or the magic duck again, but the good wife soon went to bee-keeping, which made her very happy.

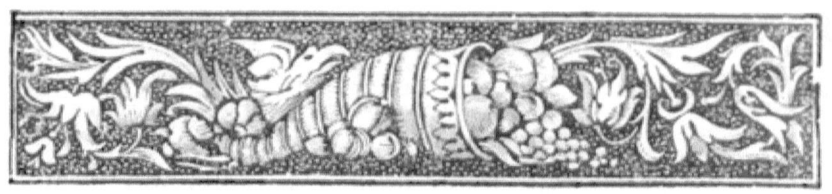

ROSY'S STAY-AT-HOME PARTIES.

"OH! dear, oh! dear," sighed Rosy, "I'm the most unhappy little girl in all the world."

She was kneeling in a chair, gazing through the drawing-room window. In the street outside was drawn up a carriage, into which Nurse was packing all of Rosy's brothers and sisters. Clover was there, a boy of twelve, looking rather disgusted with his surroundings, and having his head nearly cut off by his first upright collar. Violet, Rosy's twin sister, was there, dressed in the sweetest new pale blue camel's-hair, and taking great care to turn the skirt of it up over her shoulders as she nestled into her corner of the landau. (Rosy thought with a pang of her own new dress, the double of Violet's, hanging upstairs in the wardrobe, in a melancholy way!) Jonquil was there, the chubby, golden-haired, big-eyed brother, aged three. And last of all was dear wee Honeysuckle, like a bundle of lace and flannel in Marie's arms; while old Nurse's spectacles could hardly be seen through the mass of sash-ends and fluted petticoats, and scarlet stockings, and velvet breeches, and flying locks of hair completely filling the roomy carriage. No one could doubt that the children were going to a party, even if they had not announced that fact to everybody within ear-shot by the chatter of their busy little tongues!

At last all were settled, and the carriage rolled away. "Good-by, Rosy," "Good-by, Yosy!" came up in a shrill chorus; and, the last Rosy's tear-dimmed eyes could see of them, hands and handkerchiefs were waving a farewell to the sister left behind.

Then it was that Rosy's fortitude completely forsook her, and she dropped sobbing into the chair. It was a bitter disappointment, for the party was to be given by their aunt in honor of these children, and, in addition to Punch and Judy, magic, and a candy-bag, they were promised a huge bran-pie, full of delightful hidden presents. Rosy had suffered from a pretty bad sore-throat the night before, and the doctor had forbidden her going out. It is no use for grown people to say, dear children, these disappointments of yours don't matter much, for they *do*. They seem as high as mountains in your path, and I fully sympathize with you all, and especially with little weeping Rosy.

So thought her mamma, evidently, for she came into the room just then, and picked the little bunch of blue serge and cardinal ribbons up in her arms, and sat down with it in a low chair by the fire.

"Boo-hoo!" said Rosy, breaking out afresh when she felt mamma's kisses on her hair and wet cheeks. Mamma said very little, but by and by the little girl began to feel comforted, in spite of herself. You know how it is, dears! First, you stop roaring and moan, then your eyes are kissed dry, then you burrow your heads down and sigh, then you lie quite still for a little while—and at last, after blowing your noses in an heroic way, you are ready to laugh again!

All this happened in Rosy's case, and for awhile she sat talking, until her mamma was called away to attend to some household matter. By that time Rosy was quite content to be tucked into a corner of the comfortable sofa, covered with a down quilt, and left to gaze into the depths of a woodfire, burning gently (for it had passed the spitting, spluttering stage), upon two great old-fashioned brass andirons with claw-feet and queer round bald heads.

Around Rosy's couch was drawn a gay Japanese screen; before the fire was spread a great black bearskin rug, and on either side of it stood a tall green porcelain jar. Clover always said these vases were like the ones in which Morgiana hid the Forty Thieves, and the children had more than once stuffed baby Honeysuckle into one of them to keep her out of mischief during what Nurse called their "rampagin's to split one's head."

Over her mamma's writing-table, low enough for Rosy to look into the very heart of it, hung a picture in a broad gold frame. The picture was of a chestnut wood in Brittany, and standing in the shadow of a drooping bough was a little girl of about ten, her own age. One of the little peasant maiden's arms was clasped around the neck of a big dog, harnessed to a cart of vegetables. Under the other arm she held a fat goose with a dangling neck. Overhead, the sky was blue and the leaves seemed to be rustling in a summer wind. Around the feet of the tiny nut-brown maiden, with her odd high cap, grew tall heather and feathery ferns, with here and there a clump of flame-shaped lilies. When snow was on the ground outside Rosy always loved to gaze at this pretty scene, and to fancy herself stepping over the frame to have a chat about vegetables, and a ramble in the forest with Annette.

Rosy's eyes wandered from one object to another in this pleasant room. Fluff, her mother's Skye terrier, curled up on her feet and fell asleep. The clock upon the mantel ticked softly, Fluff snored contentedly, little particles of burning wood pattered into the bed of glowing embers below. Even the familiar rumble of the street cars along the thoroughfare at the end of their block seemed more subdued than usual; and Rosy lay, never stirring, until—she found herself, without the least warning, slipping down through one of her mother's great porcelain jars, into Japan! Fluff woke up, and dashed to the rescue, with his fierce little "Rah!" of a bark; but there was nothing to be seen of Miss Rosy except the tip of a scarlet bow, with which Nurse was wont to adorn the summit of her

young lady's head. She felt the rustle of the dried rose-leaves at the bottom of the jar falling over her in a fragrant shower, as she fell through space, pulling up, decidedly out of breath, in a very queer locality.

It was a town where the houses looked as if they had been built for big dolls to live in. Houses with sliding walls, doors, and galleries made all of paper, that in two minutes you could take apart and pack up as you do a box of Crandall's blocks. The streets were honeycombed with quaint booths, and crowded with human beings going in and out of them like bees. The carriages were babies' perambulators, drawn by a tandem team of brown-skinned men, wearing a single garment each, and umbrella hats.

There were no horses to be seen, but the cows wore blue cotton wrappers and shoes made of straw. Men, women, and children, at first sight, seemed to be dressed alike, all clattering around on high clogs, stooping painfully; and the funny little bald-headed babies were either carried pick-a-back by their mammas, or else were tucked in the breast of their fathers' loose wrappers, together with pipes, tobacco pouches, books, and a variety of other useful articles.

Rosy looked about her in astonishment, till a girl came up and saluted her with solemn politeness, inviting her to a party, which was just about to begin. "You had better have your hair dressed first," the girl said, "and I will lend you a decent frock."

"Very well," said Rosy, thinking fondly of the blue camel's-hair in the wardrobe at home; "of course, this old every-day serge won't do for a party."

The girl took her to the shop of a female barber,

who made Rosy kneel down before a mirror of polished steel, and parted her hair in two or three long manes, which were stiffened with bandoline, and tied with paper twine in a wonderful bow-knot on top. A fine tortoise-shell skewer was added, and the barberess, stepping back to survey her work, caught sight of Rosy's eyebrows.

"Tut, tut," she said, angrily; "what were her parents thinking of to let them grow like this?" And without more ado Rosy's eyebrows were shaved off, and her face and neck were daubed with a thick white paste. Her under lip had a patch of red paint, and her teeth were stained with some horrid black mixture. Then she went with the Japanese girl into a paper house, where the party was to be held, and the girl lent her a loose silk gown, tied round the waist by a wide sash of pink crêpe. On her feet were put foot mittens of white cloth, with a separate place for the big toe, and high lacquered clogs.

"How can I walk?" said Rosy, tottering around when she was finally equipped in her narrow uncomfortable garments.

"Sh-h! the company is arriving!" said her hostess; and as there was no furniture, not even a chair, Rosy wondered where the company would sit. The company solved this difficulty by sitting on the floor; and then trays were handed around, containing all sorts of wonderful sweetmeats, flowers and fruits in lovely colors, with conserved fruits, sugared beans, and candy fish, animals, and birds. Each dainty was more tempting than the one before, and Rosy found the loose front of her Japanese gown the very thing for a "party-pocket," if any of you know what that means!

Next came games; "Lady-go-to-see," "Sick man-and-doctor," Alphabet-cards, and Proverbs; and then, more sweetmeats. Pleasant as it was, a sudden stop was put to the entertainment, by a commotion, everybody seizing hold of another, all with frightened faces. Without warning, an earthquake came and turned the house upside down. Everybody fell out on the ground but Rosy, who flew up in the air, becoming entangled in the tail of a huge man-kite, carried along by the wind at a fearful rate of speed.

Rosy thought this much more exciting than any coasting down hill she had ever tried; and she flew up, up, until the tail of the kite gave a flop, tossing her through a rift in the clouds. There she was, passing again through the bottom of the porcelain-jar, and in another moment she had landed in the very centre of the bear-skin hearth-rug.

Rosy was just getting her breath, and wondering how she came to have her hair hanging in the usual tawny stream, when, to her great surprise, the bear-skin began to move.

"Hold on tight there. We are off," it said, in a low growling tone, though not unkindly. "Want to go to a party, hey? Well, I'll see what we can do for you in my part of the world."

"Really you take one so unpleasantly by surprise," exclaimed poor Rosy, as she felt herself again setting forth on an airy journey. "It is so cold here, I wish you had let me stop for my seal-skin jacket."

"Don't talk about seal-skins, child. We are going where you will see enough of them. Ho! but it's grand there, up among the icebergs and the everlasting snow-drifts, where the frozen lakes gleam like red jewels in the light of the sun that never sets! Merry sports you'll see between my brothers and sisters!"

"But I should be dreadfully afraid of them," began Rosy, trembling. "I have never met any bears outside of cages;" but the words were frozen on her tongue, and some tears coming into her eyes rolled in little round icicles into her lap.

Now they came to a world of ice and snow. Even the fir-trees were no longer seen. Clinging to the rocks was a little rough moss, which served for reindeers' food. All else was chill and glittering—the sky arched with radiant pink that seemed to palpitate. Far below them was a polar sea, locking in chill embrace a lonely ship, her shrouds sheathed in ice, her ribs cracked against the huge silvery bulk of an iceberg, on whose jagged side she leaned despairingly—no sign of life on board. Rosy shuddered and shut her eyes, only opening them again when the bear-skin set her down at the side of an odd little hut, built on a barren point of land above the ice-bound water.

This hut was made of blocks of ice, the chinks filled

in with moss, and snow-caked over all. On top was a hole whence issued a faint curl of smoke, and out of an opening, somewhere, crawled a funny Esquimaux lady, apparently as broad as she was long. She welcomed Rosy politely, and took her in to the fire, a civility Rosy thought she could have done without. The whole family was collected there, with some guests invited in Rosy's honor, who had come in sledges drawn by dogs over the snow. The dogs also were within, and half a dozen children. It made Rosy think of the worms in Clover's can the days when her brother went a-fishing, so closely packed and squirming were her new-found friends. The place was full of smoke, and smelled of fish oil. The feast consisted of frozen whale's blubber, handed around to be gnawed by the company, and of salt fish dried without cooking, with strips of reindeer meat. Rosy tried to be very agreeable to everybody present, but when they brought her the baby to kiss, she almost fainted! It was the greasiest little thing, without a stitch of clothes on! By-and-by, sleep overpowered the traveller, and Mrs. Esquimaux laid a skin before the fire, offering her, for a pillow, what *do* you think? that self-same greasy baby!

As this ceremony is an especial compliment to a stranger among the Esquimaux, no one can refuse it; and Rosy, with much compunction, laid her head down on the poor little thing, who took it all as cheerfully as possible.

Scarcely had the weary traveller closed her eyes, when she opened them again on the lounge in the drawing-room at home!

There, looking down on her with a friendly smile, was the little Breton maiden in the chestnut wood.

"Come to my party," Rosy heard her whisper; and, charmed with such a pretty new playmate, she stretched out her hands. The little French girl dropped the goose from under her arm, and leaned out of her gold frame to help Rosy, who, in two or three steps was safely beside her, treading down the tall heather, and stirring the butterflies from their haunts among the flowers. How green, and cool, and sweet it was, under the arching boughs. Far as the eye could reach, on every side, were leaves rustling in the fragrant air; and the trunks of the ancient trees were gray and hoar as the beards of the old Druids who once haunted them. Annette, for so the peasant maid was called, told Rosy many strange and interesting tales about this forest as they walked on, followed by the faithful dog dragging his cart of vegetables so carefully that he did not need a word or look to guide him.

"Ours is one of the oldest inhabited parts of France," said the girl, proudly; "I can tell you stories about every tree and rock and hill in the country-side, and I will, if you like to hear them; but we must make haste to reach the market now, before the sun rises high enough to drink the dew from my vegetables. I was up before day to pick them, and my father has promised me that, if I sell all, I shall have a party in the glen. Only think! Not to work in the field all the afternoon —and to have as many chestnuts as we choose, a whole loaf of brown bread, and perhaps—if the step-mother is good humored—a slice of seed-cake!"

Rosy thought this a very poor sort of a party; but she found Annette such good company that it seemed no hardship to trudge along the hot and dusty road beside her, when they emerged from the shelter of the wood. The two girls laughed and made merry until they reached the market town, and there the good dog came to a halt, while Annette arranged her cress and lettuces and beans and potatoes in tempting rows upon the stall—standing beside them with such a patient smiling face, that many passers-by were induced to buy of her. The fat goose went home in the basket of a fat housekeeper, and left in his place a pile of silver pieces. So, Annette and Rosy soon turned back to trudge again the dusty high-road, talking of the party they were to have in the glen that afternoon.

Annette's home, which the two tired little travellers reached at last, was a quaint cottage, the steep moss-grown roof looking twice the height of its walls. Over the door grew a twisted pear-tree, and all the ground around it, excepting the garden patch in a sheltered spot behind, was one waving mass of heather, strewn with gray boulders of mossy rock. Rosy gave a little cry of delight.

"Why, it is the *sweetest* place," she cried. "It is like a bird's nest, Annette. How happy you must be here."

Annette was about to answer, when out of the door came a cross step-mother, who began scolding as soon as she saw the girls, snatched the pouch of silver money from Annette's side, ordered her to the right and left, and then, tired as the poor child was, harnessed her to the cart beside the dog, and made her draw a heavy pile of linen to the brook, where she was at once set to work to help her step-mother in the family washing. Rosy, half-starved by her long fast, was glad to share Annette's meagre dinner of brown bread and a handful of boiled chestnuts, eaten under a tree by the brookside. Annette ventured to remind her step-mother of the promised party, and, for answer, received a smart box on the ear.

"Is it a princess I have got to do my work, perchance?" said the cross old thing. "Thy father is far enough off in the field, not here to spoil thee, by luck; so do thou and that idle girl yonder set to work and finish washing the linen. That's party enough for trapesing girls, in *my* mind!"

So Rosy, too, was forced into service, and all through the long afternoon she toiled with aching limbs. When night came, she and Annette were glad to seek a straw bed in a tiny roof-chamber and cry themselves to sleep.

"Never mind," said Annette, patiently; "to-morrow, perhaps, she may be kinder, and after we have worked all the forenoon in the field, who knows but we may have our party yet?"

Rosy remembered nothing more, except opening

her eyes full upon the hearth in her mother's drawing-room, where she was immediately addressed by one of the old-fashioned brass andirons.

"I should just like to show you what a party was in *my* time," it said, in a cracked, high-pitched voice. "We, sister Peggy and I, belonged, as you know, to your mother's grandmother—a good old Revolutionary stock—and we lived in the old house up yonder in Salem, Massachusetts, until your mother took it into her fanciful head to fetch us here. I should like to know what we have in common with that little fiddle-faddle Dresden china clock and shepherdesses upon the mantel-piece! However, I won't talk about my grievances, for sister Peggy always says that it is in very bad taste, and sister Peggy knows. We lived in the room where your grandmother was born, my dear, and her first cap was fitted upon sister Peggy's knob——"

"Will she never stop to take breath," Rosy wondered. "I am dying to ask her a question. What's your name?" she suddenly called out, so abruptly as to make the old andiron jump, and let fall a broken brand upon the hearth.

"Dear me, child, how you fluttered me!" it said, reprovingly. "I am sister Polly, of course, as you would have heard in due time. Sister Peggy always says that little girls should be seen and not heard, and sister Peggy knows—Where was I—Oh! when your grandmother grew old enough to invite her little friends to share her hospitality, the boys and girls would arrive at about three o'clock in the afternoon. The girls wore plain print gowns, and muslin aprons edged with tambour work. Instead of that insane mop of hair you sport, with a bow in the middle, looking for the world and all like your terrier, Fluff, they had decent mob caps. Their hands were covered with mittens, and each one carried a bag with a piece of white seam (or plain stitching), or else a sampler frame. How pretty it was to see them sitting down to their work for awhile! Then the tea-table was spread, with flowered china cups and plates, and shining silver, muffins, crumpets, sliced ham, home-made preserves and cream, and waffles strewn with cinnamon and sugar——"

"You make my mouth water," said Rosy.

"All this took place by five o'clock," said sister Polly, "and afterward the children had a good game of 'blind-man's-buff,' or 'hunt-the-slipper'—and a handful of nuts with a big red apple, to stuff in each of their pockets upon going home. I remember a very little party your mamma had once, when she was a child—— "

"Do you? Tell me about it, please," said Rosy, eagerly, for nothing was ever so enchanting to those children as stories about their mamma in her youth.

" She was just getting over the measles, and had been very much petted during her convalescence. Your grandmother promised her, in reward for taking a rather nasty dose of medicine, that she should have her little cousins from next door, to drink tea on a trunk. This was an especial treat to your mamma. A large flat-topped trunk served as table for the little girls and their dollies. On it were spread the china doll tea-things, and when they did not suffice in size or numbers, leaves from the grape-vine above the dining-room porch, were also heaped with goodies. Those children were satisfied with broken bits of peppermint stick, ginger-nuts, wee biscuit, lemonade for tea, and in the centre of the table a dish of horse-cakes."

"Oh, I know!" said Rosy, with much interest. "Mamma has often told us about horse-cakes, and the funny little old shop where she used to buy them for a cent apiece. They had currants for eyes, and the children never knew whether to begin to eat at the head first or the tail——"

"Exactly," said sister Polly. "Well, as I was saying, four little girls in clean white birds'-eye pinafores assembled around the trunk-party, your mamma at the head, to pour out the lemonade tea. Each guest had a dolly in her lap, and your mamma had twins on hers. I think the difficulty began by her insisting that the twins should have a double share of all the good things, which the guests, with some warmth, disputed. At any rate, it is a sad tale to tell you, but a true one; a quarrel set in, and what should the hostess do, but burst into tears, declare that her company were mean horrid things, and then, dragging at the table-cloth, whisk the entire contents of the tea-table upon the floor!"

"Oh!" said Rosy, "did my mamma do that? I don't believe a word of it! You are nothing but an old tattle-tale, sister Polly, and I don't believe sister Peggy is any better!"

Scarcely had Rosy uttered these disrespectful words, when the enraged sister Polly and sister Peggy flew out upon her from the fire-place. Seizing her in their brassy claws, they shook the little girl fiercely, bumping her head first on one side, then on the other, between their knobs.

Rosy screamed for help, and heard in return a merry peal of laughter. She felt a warm shower of kisses on her face; and, opening her eyes, saw Clover and Violet, Jonquil and the baby, mamma and the nurses, standing in a laughing circle around her couch, while Fluff nearly barked his head off in the general excitement.

"Rosy, you had the funniest nightmare!" said Violet; "see here, what a lovely bracelet was in the bran-pie for you, and we've all saved you some of our bonbons."

"It was rather a bully Punch and Judy," remarked Clover, patronizingly. "That is, for the little ones, you know; *I've* seen such lots of 'em."

"Punch said, 'Doody, Doody, bing up de baby,'" squeaked happy little Jonquil, capering about.

Baby Honeysuckle had gone to sleep, after her first party.

Rosy jumped up, and kissed everybody around twice.

"Dear knows I've had enough of parties," she declared joyfully; but nobody knew what she meant!

Queen Blondina Resting in her Garden.

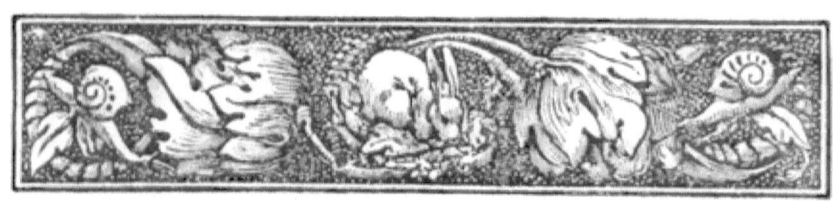

BLONDINA; OR, THE TURKEY-QUEEN.

 CERTAIN king had two daughters, one of them lovely and accomplished, and the other an ugly, cross-tempered personage, who early in life took to meddling with the black arts, and learned a great deal more of magic than she did of any thing else. Blondina, on the contrary—for so the pretty princess was named—was the joy of all her nurses, and governesses, and tutors, and music masters, from earliest infancy. Her one fault was a tendency to laugh aloud on the slightest provocation. At ten years old she could speak many languages, play on all known instruments, write essays and sermons, dance like a sylph, sing like a nightingale, and make chocolate caramel. Vixetta, the elder of the two sisters, before she had reached the same age, had made short work of *her* instructors, wearing out the health and spirits of a

governess in a week, and driving twenty-four tutors into the lunatic asylum, while her head-nurse was speedily reduced to skin and bone, and took a permanent situation as the living skeleton in a dime-museum.

The poor king remonstrated in vain with his headstrong elder daughter. Ordinary scolding had not the slightest effect upon her; black marks and crosses against her name in the report-book only made her laugh scornfully; and any attempt at bodily punishment ended in the Princess Vixetta throwing herself flat upon the ground, turning purple in the face, and foaming at the mouth with rage in a way to daunt the stoutest spirit. So, for this reason, the unfortunate girl was allowed to follow her own fancies, stealing off at dusk nobody knew whither, although it was suspected that her favorite haunts were the black depths of a pine forest near the palace—where the country folk never cared to ramble, even in broad daylight—or a certain ruined tower, filled with bats and owls and serpents. One night a peasant, who approached this tower in search of a lost cow, saw green lights dancing madly around the broken walls, heard wild shrieks of laughter issue from within, and, on venturing to insert his inquisitive nose into a chink, had it tweaked by two red-hot fingers; immediately afterward, he averred, he had seen the Princess Vixetta, in true witch-dress, shoot by him on a broomstick, leaving a trail of brimstone in her wake. On reaching home he found his sheep dead, his best cows gone dry, and his children ill of a fever. Such tales as these, of which there were many current in the country-side, came from time to time to the king's ears, and not being able to gainsay them, *because of information he had got on his own private account,* the unfortunate parent resigned himself to sink slowly to the tomb. In fact he courted death rather than shunned it. Whenever he took cold, he would sit all night long, in wet shoes, in the draft of two open windows; and if that did not make him worse, would send away the doctors, refuse medicine, and try to beat his brains out on the marble floor of the palace bedroom. At last, one day, he choked, on too large a mouthful of beefsteak, and when the phy-

.Blondina...

sicians endeavored to relieve him, waved them away, and cheerfully expired!

The Princess Blondina was immediately proclaimed queen in her father's stead. Nothing was heard but praises of the charming new sovereign, who, after the period of mourning had passed away, ascended the throne with much pomp and ceremony. All of this was gall and worm-wood to the envious Vixetta, who, but for the kindness of her sister, would have been sent, by a vote of all the people, into exile in a distant land. Blondina announced that the Princess Vixetta should remain in her palace, and be offered an opportunity to reform her bad ways. Vixetta, thereupon, pretending to weep, promised to do better, and to give up associating with her evil favorites, the witches, warlocks, and magicians; but, in secret, her time was spent in conjuring a method to get rid of her beautiful sister, and to mount the throne in her stead.

One warm summer day, Queen Blondina had just come in from rowing in her silver barge along the windings of the little river which watered the palace grounds. She rested for a while in the garden upon a bank of roses, myrtles, jasmine, and lilies-of-the-valley, while allowing her maids-of-honor to fan her with huge fans of white ostrich plumes, and listening to the drip of fountains of orange-flower water, and eau-de-cologne. Suddenly, she espied a poor old tattered crone, carrying a basket of luscious fruit, such as none of the queen's own gardens or green-houses could produce.

Pomegranates there were, dropping sweetest juices when cleft in twain, purple figs that melted upon the tongue, rosy nectarines, crimson plums frosted with silvery dew, and bunches of grapes glowing like jewels where the sunbeams touched their clusters. Queen Blondina sat up, and exclaimed with delight,

"Oh! Goody, pray set your basket down. My servants will pay you handsomely for your lovely fruit."

"Willingly, your Majesty," said the old woman. "You are welcome to the contents of my basket, if you will but leave me the single hazel-nut at the very bottom of it."

The queen consented, with a laugh at the absurdity of her wanting that one insignificant little hazel-nut, when such a delightful treat was at her service. Her servants unpacked the basket, and there, sure enough, at the bottom, was a tiny brown nut.

"Queer, that she should desire to keep back that one little nut," thought the queen. "I wonder why? Can it be so very delicious to the taste, or what? I wish I could see its inside."

And so she went on, wondering, and exciting her own imagination, till, pretty soon, Blondina would have given all the rest of the basketful for the possession of that single mysterious nut! She began by offering one gold piece, then another, till a glittering pile lay at the crone's feet, but still the old woman held out against parting with her treasure.

At last, Blondina burst into tears, when the crone appeared to be melted by her sorrow, and, advancing, whispered in her ear.

"If I give you this nut," she said, "it shall be on one condition, only, your Majesty; and that is, that you crack it in the presence of your prime minister alone, in some remote corner of your palace."

Blondina gladly consented, and sending away her attendants, took possession of the nut, and summoned her prime minister to her side. This functionary was a very stern and important officer of State, who had been foremost in the movement to banish the Princess Vixetta from the court. He arrived all breathless, at the queen's behest, and in the meantime the old crone had disappeared as mysteriously as she came. Blondina ordered the prime minister to follow her to a secluded summer-house, where, eagerly cracking the nut with her royal high-heeled shoe, she found inside only a few pinches of white powder, and a scroll containing some fine writing in an unknown tongue.

"Thanks to my love of study, your Majesty," modestly suggested the prime minister, "I have mastered the only language you have left unacquired, which happens to be Arabic. On this bit of paper, I can decipher certain instructions to the finder."

"Tell me them, quickly, my dear lord," said the enchanted princess, "and I will apply myself to the study of Arabic to-morrow. So much for a neglected education," she added, with a sigh that she had left anything so important undone; for, as I have said before, this princess had a passion for acquiring languages.

"If the finder of this treasure desires to acquaint himself with the language of the animal world, and to take the form of any other living thing, he has only to snuff up a pinch of the enclosed powder, bow to the earth three times, and cry the name of the creature he desires to become, followed by these exact words:—

'Kurri-kuree,
Changed would I be.'

"At once he will assume the likeness of the thing named, and will understand all he hears going on around him, remaining in that shape as long as he may choose. Whenever he wishes to resume his own natural form, he has only to bow himself again three times to the earth, and repeat the formula already given. But let him, during the period of transformation, especially beware of laughing aloud—or he will inevitably forget the formula, and run the risk of remaining as he has chosen to be."

"This is the most delightful thing I ever had happen to me," said the merry young queen, clapping her hands. "Come, my lord, I am dying to try the experiment. Suppose we become two turkeys, and wander into the barn-yard. Nothing could please me more than a little adventure of that kind. Besides, you forget I have never studied Turkish, and this will be an excellent opportunity."

The prime minister, who was a man of sober years, beyond the taste for such mad-cap frolics, remonstrated in vain with his wilful mistress. Blondina would have her way; and, in a short time, behold both queen and minister indulging in a solemn pinch of white snuff, and pronouncing distinctly the magic formula, while inclining themselves humbly to the earth!

At once, Blondina's gown of silken tissue was exchanged for a suit of neat brown mottled feathers, while the prime minister became just such a huge and unwieldy gobbler as would take first prize in a Christmas poultry show!

"Oh! what splendid fun!" the queen began, dying to laugh at her companion. But reflecting upon the possible consequences of this indiscretion, she became grave and silent, while the humiliated prime minister waddled after her into the barn-yard, whither his perverse little sovereign now took her way, leaving the hazel-nut securely hidden in a corner of the summer-house.

In the multitude of feathered folk assembled in the enclosure, our two turkeys passed almost unnoticed at first. They were surprised to find very much the same sort of talk going on among their new friends, as among those they had left. The same struggle for prizes and for place, the same greedy rapacity, the same love of gossip and display. Two new peacocks had that day been added to the collection, and were strutting up and down like fashionable loungers, discussing all the affairs of the nation and the conduct of the rulers; and, in listening to their discourse, the queen found herself much enlightened about many of her subjects, and their doings.

"As to her Majesty, Queen Blondina," said one of

the peacocks, sending his tail up in a magnificent fan when he saw the admiring gaze of two young guinea hens bent upon him, "I have reason to believe that this unfortunate young woman is doomed soon to fall a victim to the wiles of that powerful enchantress, her sister, who, as is well known to all of us, has just become the sovereign of the underground fraternity of magicians, against whose spells all other witches and warlocks can do nothing."

Blondina strained her ears to catch the answer; but the two talkers had passed on, and she heard a sharp voice say close beside her,

"Come now, no struggling, if you please, Mr. Mole. I have not tasted so much as a mouse to-day, and you have crossed my path in the nick of time."

"Dear Miss Tame Owl," pleaded the little velvet-coated victim, held tight in the claws of a spinster-owl, domesticated in the barn-yard by Blondina's special orders, "I must entreat you to let me off this time; I was hurrying to my daughter's wedding, and mistook the way, straying into this dreadful place by the most unfortunate mischance. Consider the feelings of my family, who are all assembled and expecting me."

"Come now, no nonsense," said the cross old thing. "My mouth is fairly watering for you."

She was about to cut short the victim's observations in the most abrupt manner by taking him bodily into her crop, when Blondina interposed, and flying at the owl, boxed her ears soundly. At this, the venerable lady was so unpleasantly taken by surprise, that she opened her mouth to gasp, and out fell the mole, who instantly scuttled away, but not without bestowing upon his turkey benefactress the most ardent thanks. After this little incident, Blondina's attention was distracted by a variety of curious studies in fowl-life, and she forgot all about her companion, the prime minister, until, chancing to look around, she beheld him the centre of an admiring throng of ducks, geese, and chickens, whose numbers were constantly increasing. "How grand he is!" "How big!" "How noble!" echoed on every side; and the prime minister, who was very vain, drooped his wings, set up his tail, and puffed himself into a magnificent fluffy ball. "Never have we beheld a turkey of so majestic a bearing!" cried a gushing goose-widow, and a pair of young lady ducklings rolled up their eyes in rapture and nodded assent. The prime minister was in his glory.

"Yes, I am indeed the champion," he said, swelling into a balloon of feathers. Just then, Queen Blondina's own pet kitten, Floss, wandered across the yard, and having no especial occupation in view, charged at full scamper upon the prime minister, who, alas! for his boasted dignity, subsided ingloriously, and, shutting himself up tight, fairly turned tail and ran away, looking so excessively crest-fallen and foolish that Blondina could not resist bursting into a long and merry peal of laughter.

"What have you done, your Majesty?" cried the alarmed prime minister, now remembering himself, as together they took refuge in a neighboring field. "Is it possible you can have forgotten; and, for my part, I saw nothing to laugh about. I never imagined a more dreadful beast than that unmannerly little pet of yours which attacked me."

The queen broke out afresh into laughter, and laughed until she cried. Then, seeing the discomfiture of the prime minister, she decided that she had for to-day had enough of the animal world, and would indulge no more in such amusements until to-morrow.

"I beg ten thousand pardons, my dear lord," she said, shaking with suppressed laughter. "But if you could only have seen yourself! Ha, ha! However, we have nothing now to do but bow three times, thus"—suiting the action to the word, "and say—Kik-kuk-kik! Dear me, what is it we must say? I can't for the life of me remember it."

The prime minister was as much at a loss.

"Perhaps your Majesty has forgotten *the price you were to pay for a laugh*," he observed, bitterly.

Blondina looked at him in blank horror. Too truly had she forgotten the formula, and turkeys they must remain!

And now, how sad their plight! In the midst of their other tribulations, hunger assailed them, and they could not eat the food provided for the rest. So they wandered into the fields and forest, picking at berries here and there; though, when evening came, footsore and weary, they determined to go back into the palace barn-yard, and see what was taking place there.

They found all the animals and fowls excited over the events of the day, and soon heard the news that Queen Blondina had died suddenly that morning, leaving a will appointing her sister to reign in her stead.

Next day a funeral took place, when the coffin was

filled by a lovely waxen image of the late queen, and was placed in the vault beside her father. The false Vixetta, dressed in mourning, had followed weeping after it.

Blondina and the prime minister now saw that they were indeed under the spell of a powerful enchantress, and resolved to travel to the dwelling of a certain wise woman in search of advice.

After a long journey, the two turkeys reached the hut of the wise woman, and told her their pitiful tale.

"Unfortunately, I have no power against Queen Vixetta since she has become the sovereign of the underground band," said the wise woman. "But, if you could gain an entrance to one of their Friday councils, you might pick up something to your advantage there." And then, as wise women speak but once in twenty-four hours, she shut the door in their faces, and left them to their fate.

Blondina and the prime minister repaired to the ruined tower whither Vixetta was wont to go on Fridays; and there, hiding behind a wall, they saw the wicked sorceress arrive and, lifting a trap-door in the cellar, disappear from sight. While they remained above, lamenting their hard fate, Blondina saw a tiny black object emerge from the ground at her feet, then another and another, till a troop of them were assembled. These were moles, and their leader, addressing the queen, informed her that he it was she had saved from the crop of the owl.

"We have heard of your distressing predicament, your Majesty," the mole added, with deep respect; "and hasten to offer our services to conduct you to the council chamber of the underground band."

Blondina thanked the mole fervently, and found, upon following him, that with his companions he had burrowed a long and beautifully smooth tunnel. Glow-worms were ranged along the sides to light the way, and every thing was arranged for her comfort. After a considerable time had elapsed, the travellers reached a gallery leading directly into a vaulted chamber where the witches and warlocks sat, each upon a cushion formed of a huge and swollen toad. In their midst, upon a throne made of serpents intertwined, sat the Queen Vixetta, around whose brow flickered a wreath of blue flames. Ah! she was a terrible witch to look upon. Blondina shuddered to remember the kisses she had often innocently pressed upon that skinny forehead and those lips of lurid red. Vixetta was in high spirits; she and her familiars hatched mischief together, and gloated over their evil doings in fiendish glee. Then Vixetta listened to the reports of each of the wicked creatures in turn; and, to Blondina's astonishment, in the narrators of these tales of witchcraft she recognized more than one of the most respected of her own subjects. Some of them were crones ancient and palsied, others were young and blooming girls Vixetta had led astray; among the warlocks were the gray-haired miller, the good sexton, and a courtier in whom the queen had placed peculiar confidence.

All were attended by

black deformed creatures, half cat, half human being. In the centre of the circle was a fire, and before it they set up the very waxen image of the queen which had been buried in her stead. Into this little imps were ordered to thrust sharp blades and needles in the region of the heart, while Vixetta pronounced a spell, at which all the others laughed rejoicingly.

"I'll warrant my lady Blondina will be cured of her love of laughing, after this—as well as of her curiosity. Long may she wander in her present shape," said the sorceress. "It was a merry trick I played her and that audacious old prime minister, who sought to do me harm."

"And what, pray, was the rhyme your Majesty bid them recall?" asked the courtier warlock, grinning maliciously.

"A simple one," replied the sorceress, "and you will remember it was once a password in our band,—

   'Kurri-kuree,
    Changed would I be.'"

Blondina almost betrayed herself in her delight. She repeated the words again and again, in mind, keeping profoundly silent until the witch-revels were at an end;

and at cock-crow the unholy gang broke up, vanishing like smoke through a trap-door in the ceiling of the vault.

"And now, dear little mole, take us back again," said the turkey-queen, who longed to breathe the free air of heaven and to break her awful spell.

"May it please your Majesty," said the mole, looking very unhappy, "there is a new difficulty. Yonder image of you which they consumed in the fire, is a fresh enchantment that dooms you to remain perpetually in the place where you now are; and I find by consultation with a friend of mine, a bat who lives in this cave, and who is the most kind and obliging person, that on only one condition can you now leave this spot, and that, I hardly dare name to you."

"Summon this bat to appear before me immediately," cried the wretched queen, who, finding that her feet were stuck fast to the earth, was truly overwhelmed, while the prime minister gave himself up to complete despair.

The bat appeared, and a more repulsive huge creature it is impossible to picture; but his voice was gentle and his manner most humble and conciliatory. He began to apologize for presenting himself before the queen, when she interrupted him impetuously.

"Quick—quick! tell me the condition on which I may leave this horrible place, where I shall die if I remain a moment longer. Who are you? why are you here? and why should we trust in you when every living thing in this foul spot is devoted to the service of the evil one?"

"I, like yourself, am a victim of, not a partner in, crime, your Majesty," said the bat, with dignity. "If you will permit——"

"But I can't stop to listen to anything," sobbed the poor little turkey-queen. "Get me into the daylight somehow or other, and then I will hear you gladly. Oh! kind Mr. Bat, forgive my unkind words; only free me from this living tomb, if it be possible."

"You have been told that it *is* possible, lady," said the bat, pathetically; "but, to be brief, since you insist upon it—only by promising your fair hand in marriage to——"

"To whom?" cried Blondina, in astonishment.

"To me," said the bat, withdrawing more into the shadows of the vault.

Blondina screamed with horror.

"Oh! never, never," she exclaimed, bursting again into tears of anguish.

The mole, the bat and the turkey prime minister consulted together in low whispers; and the last-named gentleman, addressing the queen, set before her the hopeless situation in which she now was, and urged her to accept the proposition of the bat.

"Hear me, too, fair queen," said the voice of the bat. "I swear that if you consent, you shall never regret it. Only trust me, and all will go well. In consigning me to this spot, your wicked sister, who, in my former estate desired to marry me herself, in spite of my aversion for her, swore that never should I be free from her enchantment, until a beautiful young bride should come to the rescue and promise to marry me, as I am, without asking any questions. Then, and then only, I might escape, taking my bride and her attendants with me."

"But your appearance—pardon me," said poor Blondina; "it is too dreadful for anything."

"Trust me," repeated the bat; and, in desperation, Blondina murmured a promise to be his bride.

Instantly the bat flew with alacrity into a corner of the vault, and, bringing thence a bunch of mistletoe, angelica, and mountain-ash, waved it thrice in a circle around Blondina, who up to that moment had remained as if rooted to the spot where she stood. The spell broke, and Blondina, starting joyfully forward, repeated, at his request, the same ceremony of disenchantment for the bat, as also for the prime minister; and all three of them, accompanied by the faithful mole, took their way to the upper regions without delay. Upon reaching the meadow where they had entered the underground passage, Blondina and the prime minister lost no time in running back to the summer-house, where, regaining the hidden hazel nut, they safely and joyfully resumed their own true shapes.

"And now, gentle lady," said the bat, who had flown after them, keeping his distance modestly, "I pray you to perform for me another kindly action. Close your eyes, and sprinkle me with this powder, at the same time touching my head with the witch-defying plants. Then, kindle a fire with these fagots of wood left here by your gardener, and cast me into the hottest portion of it."

Blondina shrank from the task, but, finding the bat as determined as he was calm and dignified, obeyed him without another word of protest. Aided by the now alert and cheerful prime minister, she kindled a fire upon the hearth of the little summer-house; and when it blazed high, and hot coals fell into the centre, she followed the bat's directions to the letter. Immediately there was a loud explosion; the hideous bat skin split asunder and shrivelled up, revealing a beautiful young prince, who stepped unsinged from the ring of flame, and bent his knee before the Queen Blondina. She recognized in him a playmate of her childhood, Prince Florizel, son of a neighboring monarch, who years before had disappeared from his father's court, and had been mourned as dead by his sorrowing relatives. To enchant him, in punishment for his scorn of her, had been one of the first acts of Vixetta's acquired magic; and to accomplish it, the wretched girl had bargained away her entire life to the service of the Evil One.

Blondina greeted Florizel with the utmost pleasure and assured him of her willingness to fulfil the pledge she had made to the dreaded bat-lover. They returned to the palace, and on being observed by the attendants, who, believing them to be ghosts, ran terrified away, had some difficulty in persuading people that they were alive and in the flesh. Then, what joy reigned over the palace. Quickly the news spread through the city and kingdom. The indignant people flocked around the apartments of Vixetta, who was still asleep after her orgies of the previous night, and, summoning her to come forth, declared that she should instantly be put to death in the presence of her victims. The miserable sorceress fell upon her knees, and begged for her life. Again the generous Blondina entreated that her sister might be spared; but Prince Florizel interfered, and insisted that, for the future safety of his queen, Vixetta should then and there be compelled to take a pinch of the magic powder and change herself into a bat. This was done, and the sorceress, flying from the window, was never heard of more.

Blondina gave her hand and heart to Prince Florizel, as soon as he returned from a visit to his parents, who were overjoyed to regain their long-lost son and heir. The marriage took place with great magnificence, and the royal couple lived in peace for the remainder of their long and useful lives. They would often walk in the direction of the poultry-yard, and Blondina loved to tell her husband of all the things she had heard and seen there when in her turkey shape.

But the prime minister, after he had weeded out of the kingdom certain obnoxious individuals strongly resembling the warlocks seen at the underground council, preferred to assume a dignified forgetfulness of all that had passed during his enforced experience as a feathered biped. To the latest day of his life he would always cross the road to avoid meeting a turkey-gobbler, and for the race of pet kittens he continued to maintain the most unconquerable dislike.

By the laws of the kingdom, to kill or injure a mole was made a capital offence; and once every year a little blind gentleman in a fine black velvet coat arrived at the palace to pay his respects to their majesties, who received him with every mark of favor and affection.

Shutting Agnes into the Chest.

TIMID AGNES.

ONCE there lived a poor girl whose wicked aunt treated her very cruelly. One morning, the aunt set out for a day of shopping and visiting to the neighboring town, after whipping her niece soundly (as she was in the habit of doing for exercise, every morning), and shutting up the poor girl in the garret, where a barrel of white sand had been spilt upon the floor.

"Pick up every grain of this sand before bedtime, or I will imprison you in the dark closet for a week," said the aunt as she went away.

The poor child cried so that she could not see the tiny particles; and as she sat, crying and picking up what she could feel, she heard a little scratching under the lid of the old wedding-chest in the corner. Presently, a pretty blue mouse with topaz eyes ran down the side of the chest, and came up to her. Now, if there was anything poor Agnes feared more than death, it was a mouse. The very sight of one had always made her shudder and scream and clutch at her petticoats, and climb up on chairs or tables or anything convenient.

So when she saw her visitor she gave a cry of terror, and climbed nimbly up to the top of a broken chest of drawers in the corner of the garret.

"Don't mind me," said the mouse, politely.

"I *beg* your pardon, but I'm so awfully afraid of you," said Agnes, shuddering to her toes. "I think I could endure you if it were not for your horrid tail! But you really make me creep all over, don't you see?"

"If you would only take that apron off your head, and exercise a little self-control," said the mouse, with a shade of impatience in its manner, "you would soon see that I am a very superior kind of a mouse. Come, Miss Agnes, I have watched you very often at your work here, and I have a great desire to be of service to you. But there is really no talking reason to a person hunched up on top of a chest of drawers with a pink apron over her head; is there, now?"

Agnes, hearing the mouse talk so pleasantly, made

a desperate effort to come down from her perch and

converse with the little creature. After a while the blue mouse's eloquence proved sufficient to induce her to follow it near a crack in the wall, and to peep between the boards, as directed.

There she saw a secret room, full of beautiful things—clothes and jewels—scattered on the floor.

"All these shall be yours, fair Agnes," said the mouse, "if you will carry me in your pocket for a day."

Agnes trembled with horror so that she could hardly bring herself to say,

"Thank you kindly, good Mr. Blue Mouse, but I hardly need anything new in the way of clothes, going out as little as I do. O—o—oh!" she exclaimed, catching her breath, as the mouse seemed to scuttle toward her.

"Do not fear! I am entirely too proud to obtrude my company where it is so little desired. Farewell, Miss Agnes; I leave you. But before I go, allow me to arrange this little difficulty for you."

The gallant little mouse whisked his tail (that hateful tail!), twice over the pile of sand, and at once, every grain of the shining heap, and all that lay scattered over the garret floor, flew back into the barrel.

"Thank you, kind Mr. Blue Mouse," cried the grateful Agnes; but no answer came. Her benefactor was nowhere to be seen. She looked in vain for the crack in the wall he had led her to; it was no longer in view.

When the wicked aunt found that Agnes had completed her task, she flew into a violent rage, and determined to rid herself forever of the girl. So, taking her again into the garret, she bound her hand-and-foot, tied a handkerchief across her mouth to still her cries, and, opening the old wedding-chest in the corner, thrust poor Agnes bodily into it, closing the lid with a vicious bang, and locking it with the great iron key.

"Lie there till doomsday, you tiresome thing!" said the wicked aunt, going down-stairs to eat her supper.

Poor Agnes thought she must soon die of suffocation, but just then she heard a scratching noise; four little feet scuttled over her face, and a long smooth tail whisked by her ear.

"Ugh!" groaned poor Agnes. "It's a mouse shut up here with me! Oh! why didn't she kill me, outright?"

Then little teeth began gnawing at her bandages and at the ropes that bound her, and in a few moments she was free.

"I am here, Miss Agnes; though, indeed, I won't

touch you again!" said the familiar voice of the Blue Mouse. "But if you would only trust me, and carry me in your pocket, how much I could do for you!"

At last Agnes consented to grant his wish and, trembling in every limb, she let the mouse run into her pocket. Without a moment's delay, the bottom of the chest gave way, and Agnes felt herself sinking, sinking. When she recovered her wits, which in that moment of terror seemed fairly to forsake her, there she was in a beautiful garden, filled with ladies and gentlemen walking two and two in a grand procession along a bowery path strewn with roses and carnations. Fountains played in the sunshine, birds sang on the boughs. It was a scene so gay and beautiful, that Agnes clapped her hands for joy.

"How happy I am here!" she cried.

"And happy you shall always be here," said a voice behind her.

Agnes, turning, saw a young gentleman dressed in a blue court costume with topaz buttons, and wearing in his cap a long smooth plume of blue, caught by a brilliant brooch of the same gems.

He explained to her that he was none other than the mouse she had so much feared. Condemned from childhood to remain a mouse until some fair maiden should, of her own free will, allow him to run into her pocket, the unfortunate prince had only now been released from his long imprisonment. This garden belonged to his own palace, and the ladies and gentlemen coming to meet him were his friends and courtiers.

Agnes, shedding tears of penitence over the blindness of her former prejudice, bestowed her hand upon the prince, and was happy evermore.

THE OGRESS AND THE COOK.

ONE summer afternoon, a young girl sat upon the door-stone of her cottage home, awaiting the return of her father from the mill. Her day's work was neatly done, and the tiny house, both within and without, was as tidy as hands could make it; hollyhocks and sweet-peas grew beneath the windows; the plates on the cupboard shelf glittered; and a little fire sparkled upon the hearth, where a pot of savory broth was bubbling cheerfully. On the table was set a brown loaf, light as a feather and sweet as a nut, with a bunch of grapes from the trellis above the door, and a pewter mug ready to be filled with frothing ale at the moment when the good man should sit down. Dimple, whose fingers rarely rested, plied her knitting-needles as she watched the bridge upon the road where the first glimpse of her father might be caught. By-and-by, up came an old crone, dusty and way-worn.

"Pray, my kind little maiden, give me a bit of food, and a sup of drink, for sweet charity's sake," begged the wayfarer, who looked as if she were ready to drop from fatigue.

"Willingly, dame," said pretty little Dimple; and bidding the crone be seated, she ladled out for her a generous portion of the fragrant broth.

The crone's eyes sparkled; and, seizing a great horn spoon, she despatched the broth in two or three mouthfuls, then asked for more. Dimple supplied her; and in a little while, all the broth in the iron pot had disappeared.

"Never mind," sighed Dimple to herself. "The good father will have to put up with a rasher of bacon and some eggs, to-night."

As if reading her thoughts, the crone, displaying a pair of jaws opening as wide as a cavern and garnished with ferocious teeth, said:

"I am just beginning to feel a little refreshed. If there were only such a thing as a couple of fat slices of home-cured bacon, and a brace of new-laid eggs to help a poor old creature on her way."

Dimple ran to fetch the eggs, over the laying of which her fowls had scarcely ceased to cackle in the barn. Quickly and cheerfully, she prepared a delicious dish, which the crone despatched as before. The loaf of bread followed the bacon, and a gallon of ale followed the bread. All of the grapes, plucked and arranged in a basket for market next morning, were consumed; and, when Dimple had just begun to tremble with apprehension lest her voracious visitor should devour *her* in conclusion, the crone pushed back her chair, jumped up with surprising agility and, running to the door, blew a shrill whistle.

Instantly, there came flying through the air a pair of huge vampires harnessed to a blood-red chariot. They halted at the cottage gate; and, before Dimple had time to cry out in her terror, the crone whisked her into the chariot, held her in place with a grasp of iron, and ordered the foul creatures to be off. Dimple fainted away and, when she came to herself, found that they were high above the earth, travelling with frightful speed through a thunder cloud. In vain she cried for mercy, and entreated to be restored to her father's house.

"Be silent, brat," said the furious crone, who was,

in reality, an ogress. "Know that I have for a long time been in search of just such a trig little cook-maid as you are. Ever since my husband ate up the two last, I have had the greatest trouble to induce my servants to stay with me. Besides, we are particular about our table, and rather hard to suit. I dare say, now, you understand cooking a nice plump baby's thigh to perfection, and how to prepare a dish of rosy cheeks smothered in cream, hey? But it isn't every day we are in such luck as to get fare like that. Many's the time I've had to palm off lamb chops for baby cutlets, and to swear that the pig's tails I served up were boy's fingers. Now, stop that ridiculous shuddering and crying, and listen to reason. If you promise to serve me faithfully for seven years, I'll engage to keep you out of his way, and to send you home with a fortune in your pocket."

Dimple's fright and horror had by this time completely taken away her power of speech. She sank upon the floor of the chariot in silent despair; and when they reached the ogre's castle, situated on a frowning peak of rocks, where not the most daring human foot could climb, she allowed herself without resistance to be lifted out, and thrust into a dark cavernous kitchen. There she was ordered to prepare a large pie, made of rats and bats, for the ogre's supper. While poor Dimple was thus engaged, a monstrous giant came home, and angrily asked for food. The ogress greeted him affectionately, and nine young ogresses ran to meet him and would have jumped upon his knees, but that he pushed them away and fell to scolding everybody, every syllable of his speech sounding like the loudest thunder-peal. Dimple finished her hateful task, and such was her skill in cooking that the pastry on coming out of the oven looked and smelt delicious. The giant ceased to frown as he devoured it, and smiled when he laid down his knife and fork.

Dimple makes rat pie.

"Come here, lasses, and I'll kiss you all," he said,

with rare amiability—actually bestowing on his wife's shoulder a pat of approval that would have felled Jumbo to the earth.

The young ogresses were tall and spindling creatures, as slim as young giraffes. They had pasty complexions, pink eyes, and long glistening white teeth. Dimple's business was, after she had set her kitchen in order, to go up into the nursery and put these frights to bed, each requiring to be rocked to sleep in a cradle nine feet long, and all howling like an army of pinched cats until slumber overtook them. Late at night, when all was quiet, poor Dimple would creep up to bed in a little turret room, where the wind moaned around the windows and owls hooted in the ivy so that sleep was impossible. She lay on her wretched bed and cried all night; and when day broke, she would scramble into her clothes again, and steal down stairs to her work in trembling, for she never knew at what moment the ogre might be prowling around in his stocking feet, and pounce upon her for a tid-bit. Months passed on, and one day the ogre came home in high good humor, carrying upon his back a living human being, whose feet and hands were tied and his eyes securely bandaged, while a gag in his mouth prevented the unfortunate victim from making a sound of remonstrance.

"Take this fellow to the kitchen," thundered the ogre, throwing his victim down upon the stone floor of the entrance hall with a violent bang; "see that he is in good condition for my table, and then serve him with plenty of onions in the sauce. Just as I was beginning to hanker after a young and tender morsel of human flesh, I came across this boy, following the plough. I'll warrant, I stopped his whistle quickly, when I grabbed him up! Now mind, wife, supper at sharp twelve, and don't forget the onions!"

The ogress lifted the prisoner as unconcernedly as one would handle a dead turkey and, carrying him below, threw him down upon the kitchen table, repeating her lord's directions to the cook. When Dimple recognized in the fainting prisoner an old schoolmate and neighbor of her own, Jim Hardy by name, she could scarcely refrain from a scream of rapture. But, pretending to be indifferent, she merely felt the poor youth's arms, as a cook examines the condition of her fowls for the table.

"Dear me, madam," she said, "surely you don't mean to cook this tough creature to-night? Why, I wouldn't dare to send up such a dish to my master. He would be in a fearful rage, and small blame to him. At least, allow me to fatten the bumpkin a bit."

"But what shall we serve my husband?" said the alarmed ogress. "He has set his heart on a dish of boy with onion sauce, and I dare not disappoint him."

"Leave that to me," said clever Dimple.

So she killed a lamb, and smothered it with onions, and the ogre knew no difference. The poor youth was set free, and great was his joy to find a friend in his proposed executioner. Dimple told him her story, and heard from him how long and sorrowfully her father had mourned her disappearance. Jim vowed to deliver her from the ogre; but both saw it was necessary to act with caution, at first. She was obliged to shut him up in an iron coop in the courtyard near the kitchen; and every time the old crone came into the kitchen, she went to the coop and felt and pinched the poor lad's legs and breast unmercifully.

"Surely he is tender enough to serve to-night, cook," she would say, impatiently. "Your master has an attack of the gout, and I am at my wit's end to keep him in good humor. Nothing would please him so much as a slice or two of the breast, grilled with pepper and mustard."

"Leave that to me," Dimple would answer; and she forthwith killed a pig, and served a dish so deliciously seasoned that the ogre forgot to growl, for at least an hour after eating it.

Once, while the supper was going on, Dimple and Jim crept up to listen at the dining-room door. After the ogre had drank a gallon or two of wine, he began to talk freely to his wife.

"Such a dainty dish as this you have served me deserves a reward, my dear," he said in a greasy voice, while the ogress meekly dipped some bread in the gravy as her share of the feast. "Open the closet in the corner yonder, and get me out my birdling."

What should the birdling prove to be but a tiny nightingale shining like gold! When its mouth opened at the ogre's command, "Sing, birdling, sing!"

out poured a rain of sapphires, diamonds, rubies, emeralds, and amethysts, that lay in a glittering stream upon the table-cloth.

"Take these for a bracelet," said the ogre, gathering them up in his hand, and tossing them to his wife; "and then put away my birdling, that no covetous eye may look upon this wonder of the world."

Dimple and Jim exchanged glances of astonishment, but dared not speak, as they crept silently down the flight of stairs.

Next day, the ogress came again into the kitchen to see about the supper dish for the evening, and in her zeal to prove that Jim was really ready for cooking, she bit his ear so that he could not help uttering a little squeal.

"See what you have done!" cried Dimple. "Now that the blood flows, he will not be fit for eating for another day or two. Certainly, *I* won't engage to make a savory dish of him."

"Oh, don't be vexed, cook," said the ogress, who by this time had grown to depend absolutely upon Dimple's word in such matters. "I have a salve here that will heal all wounds, and will even cause a limb that has been cut off to grow again to the body."

So saying, she whipped out of her pocket a little box of ointment, and rubbed some of it on the wounded place, which at once ceased to bleed, becoming whole as before.

"What did I tell you?" asked the crone, triumphantly. "This salve is one of the wonders of the world, and the recipe is handed down only in our family." So saying, she carefully put away the box again in her pocket.

Day after day passed, Dimple continuing to make excuses for failing to serve the coveted dainty, and exerting all her skill to cook such dishes as might make the ogress forget her disappointment. Meantime, Jim occupied his time in the coop by weaving a rope long enough and strong enough to support his weight and Dimple's while making their proposed escape down the rocky precipice on which the castle stood. Once on the sea-shore beneath, they hoped to hide in some fisherman's hut until a ship might be found sailing to their own country.

"One thing is certain, Dimple," said Jim, who was a bold and fearless fellow; "we shall not leave this place without carrying off that wonderful bird of his. Why, just to remember the dazzling stream that poured from its mouth, makes my eyes wink."

"Oh! Jim," answered Dimple, trembling. "Please, please, don't attempt such a thing. It will make our punishment ten times worse if we are caught. Besides, what hope have you of getting inside the iron closet? It is madness to talk about it. For my part, what I would like to take, is a little of that marvellous salve. Then, if we are bruised or our bones are broken on the rocks, we can make all right again———"

"Why should you forever be talking to yourself, cook?" exclaimed the ogress, at that moment bursting in, carrying a bunch of keys that clanked like fetters. "See here! No more nonsense! I'd just like to know when you propose to give us that chap in yonder, who must have eaten more than his weight in good food since he came here?"

"Very soon, very soon, madam," said Dimple, with a palpitating heart; "in a very few days he should be fit for my master's table. You know that kind of a creature takes uncommonly long to fatten."

"Hold your tongue!" cried the ogress, exploding in sudden fury, like a mine of fire-crackers, and hurling at Dimple's unfortunate head a few convenient saucepans, skewers, flat-irons, and dish-covers. Happily the thrower was of the feminine gender, and so the projectiles missed their aim; but, as Dimple dodged around in a dark corner of the kitchen, the ogress continued to scold her angrily.

"I know this," she exclaimed, "that for only one single day longer will I consent to be put off by your palavering promises and excuses. The lad is fit to kill now, if he is ever going to be; and as day after to-morrow is my lord's two thousand and tenth birthday, you must prepare a dish that shall be better than all that have gone before it. Everything is arranged for a night of celebration. Exactly at midnight to-morrow, we proceed in the vampire chariot to visit our neighbor, the King of the Ghouls, and, returning, shall expect to find the feast served punctually at cockcrow; the dear children may sit up for it, and my brother, the Ogre of the Seven Mountains, is invited to partake."

During this speech Dimple's blood ran cold, but, summoning up all her resolution, she answered calmly, "All shall be ready, madam;" and when the appeased ogress took her leave, Dimple flew to the iron coop, and asked Jim if he had heard the conversation.

"Indeed, did I, my lass," said Jim, trying to put a bold face on the matter. Then, they fell to consulting, and it was decided that the escape should be attempted that very night, as soon as the household was at rest. Midnight came, and not a sound save the thunderous snoring of the ogre family was heard within the castle. Dimple waited upon the landing, while Jim glided up to the cupboard where the nightingale was kept. As no one dared so much as lay a finger upon the giant's treasure without his leave, the door had been left unlocked. There sat the lovely birdling upon a jewelled spray, glittering so brilliantly that it shone like a lamp in the darkness. As Jim laid his hand upon it, the bird sent forth a note of silver sweetness, warning her captor to fly with all speed, if he would escape with his life from the vengeance of the ogre.

"I humbly beg your pardon," said Jim, respectfully; "I had no idea that you are a talking creature."

"Oh! I am glad of anything for a change! You must know that I am a fairy, unfortunate enough to have been imprisoned in a shape assumed for a frolic," the bird continued, greatly to Jim's astonishment. "And tired enough I am, of being a plaything for that horrid old monster, who captured me when I had just dressed for a masquerade party, in the plumage that you see. Unluckily, it is my doom to remain a slave to whosoever shall make a prisoner of me whilst I am thus attired and, also, to have to pour forth jewels at his command. You will be a different sort of a master, I am sure."

Jim hurriedly promised the fairy-bird to treat her with kindness, and hastened to place her in Dimple's keeping. They stole past the giant's chamber-door, but the creaking of a board aroused the tyrant, who sprang out of bed, roaring, "Who is there? Answer, or I will grind you to dust beneath my heel!"

Jim made no reply, and lifting in both hands a heavy iron bar with which he had provided himself, hid in an angle of the stairs.

Out rushed the giant, sputtering ferociously, fire shooting from his eyes and nostrils. Jim, under cover of the darkness, dealt him a tremendous blow upon the skull. The monster tottered, and fell crashing down the long flight of stairs, carrying Jim with him to the bottom. Dimple heard a terrible groan, and then all was silent. Feeling her way to the spot, she whispered imploringly,

"Jim, dear Jim, speak to me!"

"I'm here, Dimple," said a stifled voice, in reply;

"but this old wretch (who is as dead as a door-nail, by-the-way), has fallen atop of me, and I believe he has broken both of my legs. Ha! there, I have freed myself, but it's no use. I can't walk a step. Don't waste time on a cripple like me, lass; but make haste to slip down the rope and escape, before the ogress finds out what has happened."

"Never, dear Jim," cried Dimple, fervently. Just then a sleepy voice was heard above in the chamber of the ogress, inquiring of her husband what was going on below. Quick as thought, Dimple ran up to her.

"Oh, madam!" she said, "such an accident! His lordship has slipped upon the stairs, and sprained his ankle. You are on no account to disturb yourself to come down; but I beg that you will send him the box of magic salve without delay."

In her sleepy state, it did not occur to the ogress to wonder how Dimple, whose presence in the castle had so long been hidden from the giant, should have been chosen as his messenger. She was so anxious to enjoy her nap in peace, that, grunting out an order to Dimple to take the box from the pocket of a gown hanging upon the bed, she turned upon her pillow and was soon snoring as before.

Seizing the magic salve with joyful fingers, Dimple flew back to Jim, and applied it freely to his broken legs. Instantly, Jim sprang to his feet, stronger than before, and the friends prepared for flight. Unfortunately, in the darkness, Dimple had also anointed the dead giant's head, and to their dismay it now began to roar most frightfully.

"Wife, wife, wife, come down and seize these vagabonds!"

The ogress, turning in her sleep, exclaimed,

"Goodness! I know what that means. My husband has got into the pantry, in one of his hungry fits, and can't find enough to satisfy him. Dear me! Suppose he should devour the cook. That would be inconvenient. Coming, my dear, coming!" And springing nervously out of bed, she began to look for her dressing gown and slippers.

"Oh, madam," said Dimple, bursting again into the room. "His lordship is in haste to butcher the nice fat prisoner he has found below, and I beg that you will send him his hunting-knife, which lies upon the table."

"Is that all?" said the ogress, sinking back upon her pillow, greatly relieved. "Take the knife, child; you will find it at my elbow."

Armed with this formidable weapon, a blade so keen that it could split a hair with ease, Dimple returned to Jim, who forthwith pierced his howling enemy through the tongue, nailing him securely to the floor. This was the end of the most wicked monster who had for many grievous years afflicted mankind. All was still, at last, within the castle, when Dimple and Jim, holding fast their well-earned trophies, climbed out of the narrow window and began their perilous descent. The rope hung over the jagged rocks of a precipice rising abruptly from the sea. The sky was dark, and the sound of the hungry waves beneath was far from comforting to the fugitives. When half-way down, they were discovered by one of the vampires keeping watch upon the rampart. Uttering a discordant shriek, the vampire flew straight to the window of his mistress, and gave the alarm.

As soon as the ogress found out the escape of her treacherous cook, her anger knew no bounds. Tearing madly down toward the kitchen, she stumbled over the dead body of her lord, who lay pinned by his own hunting-knife to the floor. Her shrill cries now rent the air, and were echoed by those of the nine young ogresses, who ran out in their night-gowns, looking truly hideous, and cast themselves upon the body of their father.

"My salve, my magic salve, quick!" cried the ogress to her oldest daughter. Then, remembering to whom she had consigned the treasure, she rushed wildly off and, leaning out of the window, seized the rope with a ferocious jerk.

"Fly, my good vampires!" yelled the horrid creature, "and tear me those wretches to shreds before my eyes!"

Now, indeed, the fate of the fugitives seemed sealed. Dimple, clinging to Jim, uttered a cry of terror. But suddenly, a silvery voice came from the bird-fairy hidden in her dress.

"Have no fear, maiden. Set me free, and I promise to save you both from this awful fate."

Dimple gladly complied with the fairy's request. What was their surprise to see this tiny creature, no larger than a veritable nightingale, transform herself into a mighty eagle upon whose outstretched wings the fugitives, seating themselves securely, were at once carried with astonishing speed over sea and land, never slackening until they came in sight of their own beloved country! Rapid as was the flight of the vampires in pursuit, that of the enchanted eagle was far more rapid. The cruel foes were completely distanced, and it may be a satisfaction to you to learn that, flying homeward, in their blind rage and spite, to tell the ogress of the failure of their chase, the vampires ran headlong into a passing thunderbolt, and were instantly killed, their bodies falling upon the castle wall

THE NINE YOUNG OGRESSES

under the very eye of their despairing mistress. As it was impossible to get away from her eyrie except in the vampire chariot, the ogress and her nine daughters lived there for a year and a day, gnashing their teeth over their changed lot; and then they slowly starved to death. Her last moments in life were haunted by memories of Dimple, and the scent of imagined sauces compounded by her clever cook arose tantalizingly to her nostrils. At the very end, a fit of unwonted weakness took possession of the dying ogress, and she was heard to murmur, as if dreaming, "She was the best I ever had. Dear girl! I feel now that I could forgive her everything—my husband's death—her treachery—my children's untimely fate—my own approaching end—could I but taste her batter-pudding ere I die!"

Happily for Dimple, who was a tender and sympathetic soul, she knew nothing of the pangs that rent the spirit of her ancient foe. Our hero and heroine had been set down by the obliging fairy-bird at some little distance from their native village. There, after giving her their thanks, they at once offered to set their captive free without conditions. The fairy-bird, overjoyed at her good fortune, insisted upon singing for them a whole day, and a pile of precious gems then lay heaped at Dimple's feet, far surpassing in value those in the king's own treasury. Dimple and Jim were now rolling in wealth and, being also in possession of the magic salve which cures all maladies, felt reasonably secure of a prosperous future. Bidding the fairy goodby, they proceeded on foot toward the neighboring town, carrying their treasures in some old potato sacks begged from a roadside hut.

Jim sold a few of the stones, and with the proceeds purchased magnificent garments for Dimple and himself; then, hiring a train of servants to attend them, the two travellers returned to their own village, seated upon cushions of pale blue velvet in a crystal chariot drawn by six milk-white horses, with gold and silver harness.

At the approach of this splendid procession, all the people of the neighborhood came flocking from their houses to see the grand prince and princess, who had done them so much honor. To their astonishment, the chariot stopped directly in front of the miller's cottage, and out sprang the beautiful princess, trailing her silks and satins along the garden path, and, with a scream of delight, throwing her fair arms around the poor old dusty miller, who sat mournfully upon his deserted door-stone, rapt in thought. In a voice that all recognized, Dimple cried:

"Father, don't you know me? I am your loving child."

Next to be astonished was Jim's mother, a lone widow, who sat at her spinning-wheel as usual, thinking of the boy she had lost so many months before. When Jim appeared before her in all his bravery, the poor old thing nearly went into hysterics of delight—she had not hesitated for one moment in recognizing the face that had never left her thoughts.

Directly afterward, all the villagers were requested to proceed in a body to the church, where a splendid wedding was held. Everyone agreed that Dimple made the prettiest bride that had ever stepped from the old church porch, and no one could dispute the fact that Jim was the proudest of bridegrooms.

The newly married pair built a superb palace in a park near their native village, and also two smaller palaces for Jim's mother and Dimple's father. A large share of their wealth was spent in beautifying the homes of their friends; and, in time, the hamlet came to be known as the "Happy Valley," so prosperous and fertile had it grown. No sickness came near these fortunate villagers; and none of them ever died—thanks to the free use made by Dimple of her inexhaustible ointment.

At last reports, neither Jim nor Dimple had confided to anyone the true story of their life in the giant's castle. When people expressed curiosity as to the source of such wonderful wealth, Jim always roguishly said that Dimple had made it all by good cooking. This report, getting abroad, had the effect of inducing the girls of that country, far and wide, to go into their kitchens and learn all they could of the most useful of arts; which, perhaps, had as much as Dimple's magic salve to do with the health and contentment of the inhabitants of Happy Valley!

MISS PEGGY AND THE FROG.

(An old nursery tale told from memory.)

ONCE there lived a widow, whose only child was a pretty girl named Peggy. Peggy loved to play by the water-side with her young companions, and one day a large frog hopped out of the water and sat gazing at her with a loving smile.

"What a queer frog!" cried Peggy.

"I *am* a queer frog," he remarked, to her surprise. "Go back, Miss Peggy, and tell your mother that I want to marry you."

Peggy ran to fetch her mother to see the talking frog. When the mother came, the frog dived down

MISS PEGGY AND THE FROG.

into the water and brought up in his mouth a rich gold chain and a jewelled ring.

"This will I give the mother, and much beside," he said, laying the chain at the mother's feet; "and this ring with many like it is for my bride, if Peggy will marry me."

"Say yes, Peggy," whispered the mother, who was a covetous woman. "Of course you can't marry a frog, but you may get the gold and jewels all the same."

Peggy burst out crying, but her mother nudged and poked her in the side till she said "yes," in a very sobbing voice.

The frog bowed politely, laid the gold chain and the ring at their feet, dived down, and immediately brought up gold cups and silver dishes, with many rare jewels set into them. Peggy's mother gasped for joy as he heaped all these riches on the grassy bank. She ran up to the house, and found a basket which would hold them. While she was gone, the frog said nothing, but stood looking at Peggy and sighing from time to time. Peggy sat under a tree, and cried and sobbed. At last the frog spoke:

"Don't forget your bridegroom, Miss Peggy. This

day year I shall come to fetch you," and he hopped into the water with a splash.

Peggy's mother sold one of the cups for a large sum of money, and furnished their house all new. She bought gay clothes for herself and Peggy, and went to church quite regularly, since she had so much finery to show. Peggy forgot all about her promise to the frog, and the year passed by rapidly.

On the appointed day, however, the widow and Peggy were sitting at the table when they heard a knock at the door. They peeped out, and saw, to their dismay, the frog, dressed in a green and gold suit, and carrying a jewelled sword. Peggy gave a scream, and ran and hid in the cupboard, while the mother tripped to the door, and bade her strange guest good morning.

"I am sorry, but Peggy is from home to-day," she said.

"Oh! never mind. I will come in and wait awhile," answered the frog; and in he hopped cheerfully, and took a seat at the table. Peggy's mother was too angry to offer him food, but the frog helped himself and ate out of Peggy's plate. He stayed and he stayed, and all the time Peggy crouched in the cupboard, cramped and hungry. He stayed till night came; and at last poor

Peggy, falling asleep, burst open the cupboard door, and tumbled out upon the floor.

The frog ran to pick her up, before her mother could get there.

"You are a little late, my dear," he said politely. "But I can see very well in the dark, so we may set out at once, for my palace in the pond."

In vain did the widow beg and plead. The frog would not give Peggy up, until the poor girl herself went down on her knees and implored him to let her off for another year. At length he promised to go, if she would be ready to marry him that day year. Peggy said "yes," and off went her suitor, after having laid a purse of gold in the widow's lap.

"It might have been worse, Peggy, so cheer up," said the woman, clapping the purse in her pocket. "A year is a long time, and perhaps he will forget you."

Vain hope! That day year, Peggy was spinning beside her mother, when the frog knocked at the door. This time, he was dressed in blue and silver, and his hat had a waving plume; but he looked more hideous than before.

Peggy gave a jump, and ran up the garret stairs, and thence out upon the roof of the cottage, where she clung to the chimney in despair. The mother opened the door, and said she was sorry Peggy was from home. The frog replied that he did not mind, but would wait for Miss Peggy to return.

He sat in Peggy's chair; and this time he would not eat, but only sighed and sighed. Presently it began to rain and hail, and thunder and lighten dreadfully; and poor Peggy on the roof was frightened out of her life. She crept into the chimney, and soon a great clap of thunder sent her flying down into the room where her frog-lover sat.

"You have an odd way of coming into the house, my dear," the frog said; "but I don't mind, if you are ready to go now. It rains hard, but I am used to water, and you must become so; so come along."

He offered her his arm, but Peggy cried and implored to be let off. She went down on her knees to him, and at last he went away, giving her another purse and another year of freedom.

Next year, the widow and Peggy barred and double-locked their doors. The frog appeared, dressed in white and gold, but it was of no use for him to knock and call. No answer came, and he went off sadly. Peggy and her mother rejoiced at getting rid of the persistent suitor, and sat down to supper merrily, without, however, unlocking their door.

Presently, they heard a noise, and looking out saw a great army of frogs coming up the hill. The frogs formed themselves into a column and, aiming for the window, jumped through the glass, and landed on the floor. They seized Peggy, and very gently carried her out of the door and down the hill. Peggy fainted, and knew nothing till they stopped on the edge of the pond.

The widow came running down the hill just in time to see the frogs plunge into the water with her child.

Peggy sank—down, down—until she reached a beautiful grotto, where, on a throne of coral and shells, sat her frog-lover. He looked at her reproachfully, and said:

"If you had not three times deceived me, Peggy, I should not have carried you off in this way. Now that you are here, try to be resigned to me, and say that you will be my wife."

"Never, never," screamed Peggy; "you are so horrible to look at with your goggle eyes."

The goggle eyes filled with tears as Peggy spoke, and the frog shook his head mournfully.

"I see that it is of no use," he said sorrowfully, and ordered Peggy to be taken to a beautiful sea-garden, where she lived and amused herself for a long time, gradually forgetting all about her home on land. Every evening the frog came and talked to Peggy through a wall of white coral; and in time, she grew so fond of listening to his voice, that if he was a minute late she would cry for him to come.

Once when it was rather dark, the frog asked Peggy if she could bear to look at him again. Peggy said yes, and he appeared before her. Somehow he did not seem so ugly as before, and when, in a trembling voice, he invited her to sit upon his knee, she at once did so. Instantly his leg broke with a loud snap; and, as poor Peggy sprang to her feet in great remorse, she beheld, instead of her frog suitor, a beautiful young prince, holding out his arms to her!

The prince told her he had been bewitched by a frog godmother, who condemned him to remain in that horrid shape until a young girl could be found who would either consent to marry him or sit upon his knee. Peggy was very glad to have such an ending of her adventure. So they were married at once, and were then very happy. When they went back for a wedding visit to Peggy's mother, they found she had taken all the gold and silver and moved away to a distant country; and they never saw the wicked woman more.

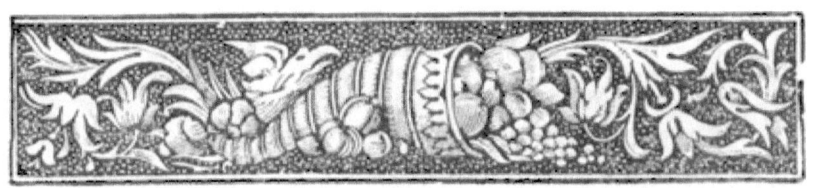

THE LEPERHAUN.

A Legend of the Emerald Isle.

ONCE upon a time, by the glimmer of the nursery-fire, a little girl sat listening to the tales told by her buxom Irish nurse. The details of most of these—notably of one very thrilling legend of the Banshee, who has ever since seemed to float upon the wind that blows after nightfall—have passed from memory; but the good old story of Molly Jones and the Leperhaun remains, and, as best I can, I reproduce it here.

In a comfortable farm-house upon the outskirts of a small village in Ireland, lived a farmer with his six sons. He was a prosperous man, and, besides having better cows, pigs, and potatoes than any other man in the county, was said to keep a tidy bit of money laid away in bank. Only one maid-servant did the work of the house, and she had lived there for many a year. At last she died, and the farmer looked about him for a girl to take her place. The wages were high, and a strapping lass named Mary Jones made up her mind that she was the right person for the situation. The farmer liked her looks, and engaged her on the spot.

"Now, Molly, lass," said the master, when he had finished taking her around the house, and showing her how neat and convenient everything was; "you see what you've got to do, and that's the end of it. Nobody in this house, who works well, has ever cause to want for encouragement, for *there's hands to help them that aren't too curious!* The main thing you'd better guard against is takin' notes and askin' questions."

Molly protested that she was innocent of the inheritance of Mother Eve; and the farmer went on with his directions.

"On the first night of every month the family goes early to bed, and it will be your business to see that the hearth is well swept, and fresh turf laid upon the fire, and to collect around it all the worn or broken shoes about the house. The last thing before you leave the room, be sure to set before the fire a nice bowl of mealy potatoes bursting from their jackets, a couple of herrings broiled to a turn, and a jug of sweet buttermilk—and, whatever you do, never forget the salt!"

Molly, though burning with curiosity, courtesied, and said nothing. All went well till the first night of the coming month. When the family was retiring, the farmer whispered:

"Remember, Molly! Be abed and asleep before the clock strikes twelve; and *don't forget the salt.*"

Molly tidied her kitchen, swept the hearth, arranged around it all the worn and broken shoes in the house, her own Sunday pair included; and, after setting a nice little meal, covered with a white cloth, near the fire, wound up the clock and went to bed. Next morning what was her surprise to find not only all the boots and shoes neatly mended, but the empty jug and platter washed and restored to their places, while a beautiful fire was blazing merrily! She dared not ask any questions of the farmer or his sons, and no one appeared in the least surprised by what had occurred. That month her work went so easily that Molly thought it child's play. Her bread was baked brown and light, her potatoes were a triumph, her churning was done sooner than anybody's in the place, and her linen was hung out to dry by sunrise on Monday mornings. For a month or two Molly never failed to set her kitchen in order, as before, for the mysterious guest. But one night she was in a hurry, and forgot the salt. Next morning the boots were mended, but the fire was

scattered on the hearth, ashes lay all about her neat kitchen, and the dishes were left unwashed. This excited Molly's curiosity anew and, when the next time came, she did everything as usual, but, instead of going to bed, hid behind the kitchen clock. Punctually as the clock struck twelve, out popped from behind a big stone in the chimney-place a queer little dwarf dressed all in red. Apparently he suspected something, for he sniffed and peered into the darkness of the kitchen. Molly held her breath through fear, and the dwarf proceeded to blow up the fire and warm himself before sitting down to supper. Then, uncovering his cup and platter, and finding that all was to his taste, he smacked his lips, and made an excellent repast. When it was over, he whipped out of his bag some shoemaker's tools, and went to work to patch and mend the shoes, with twinkling fingers. In an hour's time all was finished and, after putting the room to rights, the dwarf took his leave.

Molly told nobody that she had seen the veritable Leperhaun, the famous shoemaking fairy; but the next month she happened to be in an ill humor and hungry; so, without stopping to think of the consequences, she ate his supper herself—leaving upon the platter only a heap of potato-skins and the bones of the well-picked herrings.

That night, while all the world was asleep, in came the Leperhaun and, finding the trick that had been played on him, flew into a terrible rage, scattered the boots and shoes over the floor, broke the crockery and, seizing a broom, swept all the ashes out upon the kitchen floor. Molly, who was watching, ran up to the garret and, jumping into bed, pulled the clothes over her head in a cold perspiration with terror. But hark! on the steps outside came the pit-pat of little feet. In rushed the offended house-fairy. He seized Molly by the hair of her head, and dragged her down the stairs, and over the flags of the yard, saying,

> "Molly Jones! Molly Jones!
> Potato-skins and herring-bones!
> I'll break your bones upon the stones,
> Molly Jones, oh! Molly Jones!"

In vain Molly cried for mercy. The farmer and his sons were fast asleep, and not a soul heard her. All night long the Leperhaun dragged her about; and when the cock crowed he vanished, leaving her bruised and sore upon the threshold of the door. More dead than alive, Molly crawled up to her bed, where she lay black and blue for many a day.

The farmer, suspecting what lesson had been taught her, said nothing; and we may be sure that, when the next time came for the visit of the Leperhaun, the little red dwarf had no fault to find with Molly.

[*The stories here following are, it is hoped, so rendered, from metrical romances of the Middle Ages, as to be adapted to the taste and understanding of youthful readers.*]

THE TRIALS OF SIR ISUMBRAS.

(*From Ellis' Abridgment of the MS. in Caius College.*)

ONCE upon a time there lived a knight so handsome, so rich, and so valiant that all eyes were turned upon him. His name was Isumbras, and fortune had given him everything that the heart of man could wish for. He had a splendid castle, surrounded by vast forests, where every day he went hunting or hawking; and so generous he was with his wealth that the poor flocked to him from every quarter and never went away empty-handed.

Sir Isumbras had a beautiful wife and three lovely

sons to share the blessings of his lot; but one thing he had not, and that was an humble spirit. He forgot to own the Giver of good things, and took it as a matter of course that his life should flow on in ease and luxury.

One day when mounted on his favorite steed, surrounded by his dogs, and having his hawk on fist, Sir Isumbras cast up his eyes to the sky, and there saw an angel, who reproached him with his pride, announcing that Heaven had in store for him a speedy punishment.

Sir Isumbras fell to his knees in prayer; but hardly had the angel vanished from his sight when, on remounting his horse, the noble creature fell dead beneath him; the hawk dropped lifeless from his fist; and the faithful hounds expired in agonies at his feet. Hastening on foot to his castle, he was met by a servant, who informed him his horses and oxen had been suddenly struck dead by lightning, and that his fowls had all been stung to death by adders. Next came forward a page, who told him the castle was burned to the ground, many of his servants had perished, and that his wife and children had taken refuge, half naked, in a thorn-bush close at hand. Sir Isumbras hastened to the aid of his beloved family, stripping himself of his scarlet mantle and his surcoat to clothe them. He embraced them fondly, and thanked heaven that, though all the rest of his treasures were taken, these remained. He then proposed to his wife that, as a sign of repentance for their sins, they should all go on foot to the holy city, Jerusalem, begging their

bread from land to land. He cut with his knife upon his bare shoulder the pilgrim's sign of the cross, and then the afflicted family set forth on their travels.

Long they journeyed, eating crusts when they could

beg them, or berries from wayside bushes, until, faint and weary, they reached a broad but shallow stream. Taking his eldest son in his arms, Sir Isumbras bore him across the river, and placed him beneath a bush of broom-plant, bidding him play with the blossoms until his father's return. Scarcely had the knight left his son, when an enormous lion burst from a neighboring thicket and bore away the child. In like manner the second son became the prey of a fierce leopard; and the poor mother, who saw them so cruelly torn from her sight, fainted away, with her baby on her breast. Sir Isumbras bowed to the will of God; and when his wife revived they journeyed on to the shore of the Greek sea. Here they stood, and, through eyes that were full of tears, saw a great fleet of three hundred ships coming toward them. This was the navy of a famous heathen king, and no sooner had he landed than the travellers, who had not touched bread or meat for seven days, hastened to implore his charity. The king soon observed the robust limbs and tall stature of the husband; and perceived he was a knight in disguise, and that the wife, whose beauty was as "bright as blossoms upon tree," was, in spite of her ragged clothes, a lady of high degree. So, affecting to treat the poor couple with respect, he offered them gold and treasure if the knight would renounce Christianity and consent to fight under the Saracen banners. This offer was at once declined, and the angry king made up his mind to revenge himself by carrying away the knight's wife. So, upon an order to the attendants, a purse of gold was pressed into the knight's hand, his infant son was put into his arms, he was hurried ashore, cruelly beaten by the king's servants, and, when he recovered himself, saw a heathen ship, with his wife on board, set sail for Africa.

Sir Isumbras clasped his only remaining treasure to his heart, and followed the vessel with his eyes until it vanished from sight. Night found him still there, until father and babe fell asleep upon the bare ground, too weary to keep awake. Sir Isumbras had laid the fatal present of the heathen king, the purse of gold, in the scarlet mantle which he wrapped around his child. Scarcely had the next day's sun risen upon the earth, when an eagle, attracted by the red cloth, darted down, carrying off mantle, child, and purse in his talons.

The poor knight was at last in utter despair. He fell on his knees, and offered what remained of his life to the God he had offended. Just then he heard the noise of a blacksmith's forge, and saw, not far off, some men at work. They took pity on him and fed him. He entered their service, and bound himself for seven long years to learn their trade. During this time he forged a complete suit of armor for himself, being determined at the first opportunity to take up arms against the Saracens, whose king had not only done him such a cruel wrong, but was oppressing God's people.

At length his opportunity came. The Christian army was to fight the Saracens on a field not far from the forge. Sir Isumbras buckled on his awkward armor and, mounting a horse that had been used by the smith to carry coals, proceeded to the field of battle.

His heart beat with wild joy when he saw the foe before him. Uttering a fervent prayer, he dashed into the thick of the combat, attracting all eyes at first by his sorry steed and rough armor, and again by the splendid skill and courage of his charge. Early in the action his horse was killed under him, and the Christian chiefs made haste to present him another one, also a suit of armor more worthy of the heroic soldier he had proved himself to be. All that day the battle raged.

By nightfall Sir Isumbras, single-handed, had killed

the heathen king and many of his followers. But he was himself sorely wounded, and when brought for reward before the Christian king, and asked his name, could hardly falter out, "I am a smith's man, sire." The king swore a great oath to make a knight of this valiant "smith's man"; and, with all honor and tenderness, Sir Isumbras was carried into a nunnery, where the good sisters nursed him until he recovered from his many wounds.

Sir Isumbras was not satisfied to remain quiet long, though he had slain the heathen king. He went to the Holy Land, and for seven years wandered about a pilgrim, as before, sleeping upon the ground by night, and vainly seeking tidings of his wife by day. Once, during this time, when he was starving upon the banks of a stream, there appeared to him a cheering visitor.

> "And as he sat, about midnight,
> There came angel fair and bright,
> And brought him bread and wine.
> He said, "Palmer, well thou be!
> The King of Heaven greeteth well thee;
> Forgiven is sin thine."

Very soon after this miraculous event Sir Isumbras found his wife, who had dwelt, holy and charitable, in a

THE TRIALS OF SIR ISUMBRAS.

secluded castle, where she had been shut up by the Saracen king. She welcomed him with rapture, and together they shed many tears over their lost children. They lived together for some years, until Sir Isumbras was again summoned to do battle with the Saracens, who had determined at all cost to kill him. The fight was again hot and long, and just when Sir Isumbras was about to be overpowered by numbers of the enemy, three new champions appeared in the field, declaring themselves on the side of the Christians. These were three splendid knights, the first mounted upon a lion, the second upon a leopard, and the third upon an eagle. The Saracen cavalry, terror-stricken at sight of them, dispersed in all directions. But flight was in vain; three and twenty thousand unbelievers were soon laid dead upon the plain by the lion, leopard, and eagle, fighting with tireless fury, and driving all before them, until the entire heathen army was utterly put to rout. Then, coming back to Sir Isumbras, the three champions knelt before him, announcing themselves his long lost sons, mercifully protected and befriended by the savage creatures by whom they had been carried off. Sir Isumbras embraced his valiant sons, and led them to their mother. The Christian king enriched the entire family, restoring them to their former rank. And now wealth, titles, honors, and all that he had lost, came back to Sir Isumbras, and the remainder of his days was spent in blessed peace.

> "They lived and died in good intent;
> Unto heaven their souls went,
> When that they dead were.
> Jesu Christ, heaven's king,
> Give us, aye, his blessing,
> And shield us from care!"

BISCLAVERET.

(From one of Marie's Lays.)

ONCE upon a time there lived in Brittany a baron who was handsome, wise, courteous, and brave. Although admired and beloved by his neighbors, he remained single until late in life, when he fell desperately in love with a young lady, who did not hesitate long in accepting the offer of so distinguished a suitor for her hand. They were married, and the bride returned from her honeymoon to take up her abode in her husband's fine castle.

For a little while all went well, until the lady discovered that her husband was regularly absent from home during three days of every week. Overwhelmed with curiosity to know where he went, and how he was occupied during this time, she used every means in her power to coax the secret from him.

"Do not ask me," said her kind lord; "rest assured that I have good reasons for my conduct. If you know what takes me from you, it will only be to hate and scorn your husband, and to ruin the happiness of our life."

The lady persisted, going from coaxings to prayers and tears. At last the poor baron gave way, and confided to her that, owing to a cruel spell cast on him at birth, he was during half the week a Bisclaveret, or Man-Wolf, taking on the body of a wolf, but keeping his own feelings and intelligence as a man. Upon hearing this dreadful story, the lady fainted away. Henceforth, although her husband was more loving than ever, she was filled with horror and loathing of him; and soon she secretly resolved to destroy the monster and enjoy his wealth.

By watching his movements she ascertained that when the baron became a wolf he left his clothing in a deserted chapel on the edge of a certain wood; and she formed a plan to seize and hide the garments. So long as the Bisclaveret was without his man's clothes, he was condemned to remain a brute.

Accordingly, when, after his melancholy ramble through the woods, the Bisclaveret went one night to resume his clothes, they were gone; and, in agony of spirit, he knew that he was betrayed by his wife. He took himself off to the forest, and was there lost to human sight.

Meanwhile the wicked wife, announcing that her husband had died while on a journey to some foreign land, enjoyed his wealth and his castle. A year later, the king went hunting in the forest, and, after a stout chase, had nearly run down the unhappy Bisclaveret, when that persecuted beast, bounding from his thicket, fawned upon the king's feet, shedding real tears and uttering almost human cries for mercy. The king, struck with compassion, ordered his dogs to be whipped off, and had the strange animal conveyed with care to his palace. Bisclaveret soon became the royal favorite. He slept on a couch of soft furs, ate from a golden dish, and returned with gratitude the caresses of all who noticed him.

His gentleness and sagacity won for the man-wolf the right to roam wherever he desired to go, unchained. One day the king gave a splendid entertainment, to which were invited all the lords and ladies of the land. Among them, dressed in silks and satins, and sparkling with jewels, came the false wife. No sooner did Bisclaveret espy her chatting with the king's guests, than, to the surprise of all present, the usually mild creature rose up, growling horribly and, springing upon the lady, bit off her nose. Bisclaveret was seized, and would have been speedily killed, but that he again fawned upon the king's feet, moaning and weeping as though he longed to speak. The king ordered him to be put into a cage, and consulted with the oldest and wisest man in his kingdom, as to what could be the meaning of the wolf's sudden fury toward this lady.

"Brittany is a land of wonders, sire," said the aged man. "The lady who was attacked is as well known for a bad name as your favorite animal is for a good one. Who knows what became of her late husband, the baron? Perhaps this poor brute was beloved by that gentleman, and has some secret wrong to avenge. At any rate, you should at once shut the lady in prison until she is made to tell all *she* knows about the matter. Mayhap it is more than we suspect."

The king followed his counsellor's advice; and, when the lady found herself likely to be kept a prisoner, she preferred speech to silence. With tears of professed penitence, she confessed all, and the king lost no time in sending for the clothes of the late baron, and placing them in the cage of Bisclaveret. At first the animal seemed indifferent, and surveyed them listlessly. "Leave him to himself, sire," said the wise man. "Above all, set him at liberty in a chamber suitable to his rank. Then we shall see a wonderful change, I promise you."

This was done, and in the morning the king ran impatiently to the chamber of Bisclaveret. There, on the bed, dressed in his clothes and sleeping sweetly, lay the baron. When his royal master entered, the sleeper woke and, bending his knee before his sovereign, poured forth his joy and gratitude.

As for the wicked wife, her estates were taken from her and restored to her husband, while she herself was sent into perpetual banishment. Most people would think she had been sufficiently punished by the loss of her nose, which never grew again!

Tournament in honor of the Princess of Bealm.

ROSWAL AND LILIAN.

(From a Scottish Romance of the XVIth Century.)

THERE lived once, at Naples, a king and queen whose only son, Roswal, was a paragon of beauty and of valor. The boy, who was as generous as the day was long, did not at all resemble his father, for the king was harsh and cruel, and slow to forgive his enemies.

In the prison of the king's palace were confined three noblemen, who, having been suspected of plotting against the crown, were doomed to be imprisoned for life, and had the most cruel treatment lavished upon them every day. Roswal could not bear to hear their groans and sighs arising from the dungeon, and one day conceived the bold project of taking the prison keys from under the king's pillow while he slept, and setting the three poor sufferers at liberty. This was done, and Roswal restored the keys to their place without having been detected.

When it was found that the prisoners had escaped, the king grew furiously angry. In vain the head jailor and his assistants declared their innocence in the matter. Their lives would have been instantly sacrificed to the king's wrath, had not Roswal boldly come forward and confessed that he alone had freed the prisoners.

At first, the king vowed that Roswal should die for having defied him; but the prayers of the queen, and perhaps the cool bravery of his son in confronting him, moved him to relent. He decided to change Roswal's sentence to banishment for life to a distant court, where he was to be placed at the service of the King of Bealm, with recommendation to make a soldier of the lad, henceforth a stranger to his home.

Roswal set out on his journey to the court of Bealm, attended only by the high-steward, an envious and ambitious man, who hated the prince and would gladly have done him evil.

The king, at parting with his son, had given him a letter of introduction to the King of Bealm; and the fond mother had come secretly to press all the gold and jewels she had, a fortune in themselves, upon her beloved Roswal. Except for parting with his mother, Roswal did not feel very sorry to set out thus from home. He longed to see what marvels the wide world contained, and the memory of the three brave men he had loosed from their vile bondage cheered him in spite of his father's anger.

The high-steward was full of projects of his own; and one night, when they had stopped to rest by the side of a rushing torrent, and Roswal had plunged into the crystal stream, as he loved to do, the wicked steward seized him unawares, held him under water till he was half strangled, and spared his life only on condition that Roswal would pledge himself to give up all the money and jewels, his letter, his horse and sword, and furthermore swear never to reveal the affair to mortal man or woman. Roswal, seeing that he could not help himself, submitted, and the false steward, laughing maliciously, put spurs to his horse, leading Roswal's steed behind him, and soon disappeared from view with all the treasures.

Roswal found himself alone at nightfall in the forest, as hungry as a hawk, and very much at a loss where to find food and shelter. He wandered along till he saw a little brown hut, under the branches of a wide-spreading oak-tree. Here, in the door, sat an old woman knitting, and Roswal's youth and beauty soon won his way into her affections. She led him into her house, gave him a good meal of brown bread, eggs, honey and milk, and a bed of clean straw. Roswal slept as sweetly as ever he had done on his golden bedstead and his pillow of down at home. Next day, he offered to work for the old woman, and set to cutting up wood and binding fagots cheerfully. For several months he lived thus, until the chamberlain of the King of Bealm chanced to pass that way. Taking a fancy to the handsome youth, he carried him off to court, where Roswal was appointed cup-bearer to the king's lovely daughter. His duties were light, and the princess was kind; so Roswal had little to complain of, until one day he heard it announced that Prince Roswal, of Naples, was about to wait upon the King of Bealm and demand his daughter's hand in marriage.

Roswal pricked up his ears at this, and immediately suspected the supposed Prince of Naples to be none other than his late travelling companion, the wicked steward; though, when he heard the princess say to her maidens that this Prince Roswal was remarkably pushing, considering that he had only recently presented a letter of introduction to them, and that, for her part, she could not see what her papa found to fancy in the young man, Roswal rejoiced. He was delighted to find that the princess did not care for the impostor. Then he remembered his oath, never to reveal what the steward had done to him, and his spirits fell again.

In a day or two, the King of Bealm announced to his daughter that he had accepted the offer of the King of Naples' son, and that preparations for their marriage would immediately begin. The princess was very unhappy, for she had taken a great dislike to the pretended prince. Roswal met his late servant face to face at one of the bridal feasts, and the eyes of the steward fell before his scornful gaze. But he knew that he was safe in trusting Roswal's honor not to tell the secret, and so carried on his impudent pretence.

A tournament, lasting three days, was announced in honor of the wedding, which was soon to come off. Roswal found the Princess Lilian in tears about that time and, while endeavoring to console her, let her know, without intending it, that he, too, had fallen in love with her. This made the pretty princess so happy, that she confessed to Roswal she had loved him secretly ever since he was chosen to be her cup-bearer. She was sure he was of noble birth from his manners and appearance; and she urged him to admit that he was as worthy of her rank as of her love.

Roswal was never so sorely tempted to reveal himself! He restrained the impulse to confess by a strong effort, and, alone and melancholy, wandered out into the forest—longing for an opportunity to enter the lists of the tournament and prove his knightly skill before the king and princess; and while he sat musing thus, there approached him a knight leading a magnificent white war-horse, on whose saddle was suspended a suit of splendid armor.

"Prince," said the strange knight, bowing low before him, "put on this armor, and mount this steed.

The tournament has begun, and thou wilt be in time to prove thy prowess. I await here thy return."

Roswal said he had led his hounds to the forest, intending to hunt a deer; and so the knight offered to hunt in his absence and keep the game for him. How his heart beat with joy and pride when he found himself once more mounted on a noble steed, and clad in knightly armor! Thanking the stranger fervently, he put spurs to his horse, and galloped off.

Entering the barriers, Roswal overset all who opposed him, and then, with a tremendous rush, charged at full speed upon the false prince, who was riding up and down with a great show in the presence of his lady. The steward recoiled in terror; but the unknown knight as suddenly checked his horse, turned around, saluted the company with the utmost grace, and vanished, as he had come, like a meteor.

The company applauded, and the old King of Bealm cried out that he would give an earldom to find out who was the unknown knight.

That evening, while all the palace was ringing with accounts of the brave stranger, Roswal came home from the forest, laden with venison and followed by his hounds.

The Princess Lilian called him to her side, and told him of the events of the day. It was evident that she wished to inspire Roswal with a desire to break a lance in her behalf; but he appeared to be indifferent, and she ended in a burst of tears.

Next day, when Roswal went again with his hounds to the forest, a second knight, leading a silver-gray war-horse laden with armor, appeared and repeated the kind offer of the day before. Roswal again entered the lists, and found the steward impudently advancing to meet him. Roswal unhorsed half a dozen of the bravest riders, then, with all possible ease, sent the steward to the ground with such a terrible crash, that the miserable impostor lay as if dead for some time. The unknown knight glanced up at the Princess Lilian, and saw a look in her face as if she suspected him. Then, quickly retiring from the ring, Roswal reappeared as before, at evening, with the spoils of the day of hunting. Lilian, who was ready to declare that none other than her handsome young lover could have been the stranger knight, was much perplexed when she found Roswal quietly at home engaged in his usual occupations.

On the third day, Roswal was mounted and equipped

in a similar manner. He had a bay horse, a red shield, green armor, and a golden helmet. He cast down all of the other competitors, broke two of the steward's ribs, threw a gold ring into the lap of his lady-love, and rode away like a flash. Returning to the wood, he was met by all three of his friends, the knights who had helped him. They revealed themselves, and Roswal found to his delight that they were the three noblemen he had released from his father's dungeon. They told him they were well aware of all he had suffered for their sakes, and were prepared to befriend him still farther.

Next day had been fixed upon for the wedding, and all the court was called together in a magnificent hall, to see their king bestow their princess' hand upon the Prince of Naples. Pale and tearful, for she had cried all night, appeared the princess. She was dressed in white satin, with a silver train, carried by ten little pages in blue, and on her head she wore a diadem of immense diamonds. The bridegroom, who had been patched up by the doctors, sat, anything but cheerful, in a golden chair beside the king. Behind a group of court ladies and gentlemen stood Roswal, handsomer than any one present, and looking every inch a prince, though he wore a plain brown velvet suit, with a gold chain round his neck, the livery of Princess Lilian's household. Suddenly visitors were announced, and in came three richly clad strangers, scattering money among the servants, which made it an easy matter for them to move along.

The king received them courteously, for he recognized three noblemen of the kingdom of Naples he had known long before.

"You will be glad to salute your prince," the king said, when he had greeted them, "and to be present at his nuptials."

The noblemen refused to notice the steward, whose knees knocked together with fear, for he saw he was on the brink of exposure. The three strangers looked about them and, espying Roswal, ran up to him, fell on their knees and kissed his hand, hailing him as the true Prince of Naples. The steward, in terror, dropped upon his knees before Roswal and confessed all, drawing from his pocket the casket containing the queen's jewels, which he had been about to present to his bride. Roswal would have dealt gently with the contemptible wretch, but the angry old King of Beahn declared that he and his daughter should not be made sport of, and the offender live to tell it. So the steward was hanged forthwith, and Roswal, owning his love for Lilian, was made happy by promise of her hand— he had already won her heart, as you know.

That same day arrived news of the death of the King of Naples, and the recall of Roswal to the throne. He was married to Lilian; and it is certain that no one who had befriended him in his days of poverty was ever forgotten by King Roswal. The good old woman in the forest was enriched, the three noblemen were restored to their estates and fortunes, and Roswal's mother was made happy by a speedy reunion with her son.

> "So Roswal and Lilian sheen,
>   Lived many years in good liking.
> I pray to Jesu, heaven's king,
>   To grant us heaven to our ending.
>   Of them I have no more to say:
>   God send them rest until doom's day!"

ELIDUC AND GUILLIADUN.

(*From one of Marie's Lays.*)

ELIDUC was a knight of Brittany who, through the cabals of enemies, fell under the displeasure of the king and was banished from his dominions. Sir Eliduc did not wish to forsake his country, still less did he wish to part with the fair Lady Guildeluec, to whom he was solemnly betrothed. But the king's order was law; and, taking a fond leave of his promised wife, while vowing ever to be faithful, Sir Eliduc called to him ten of the bravest of his followers, and set sail for the English coast. They had a short voyage with fair winds, landing at Totness, in Devonshire, and proceeded at once to Exeter. The King of Exeter was at that time plunged into a most distressful war with a neighboring province, to whose prince he had refused to marry his only daughter and heiress. Sir Eliduc offered his services to the king, which were gladly accepted. After a few days a battle was fought, in which Eliduc's knowledge of the art of war and his bravery, as well as that of his ten followers, helped to decide the fortunes of the King of Exeter, who had the satisfaction of seeing the foe put to flight. As a reward for his aid, the king made Eliduc the supreme commander of all his armies. Eliduc was the idol of the people, and soon the fair Princess Guilliadun fell in love with him, confiding to the king, her father, that she would have no other husband than this valiant stranger. The king thought he could do no better than secure such a noble successor to his throne, and sent his chamberlain to inform Eliduc of the honor in store for him. Eliduc was now in a sad plight. He thought of his absent Guildeluec, who was no doubt, even then, waiting and weeping for his return, and his heart grew heavy within him. On the other hand, the Princess Guilliadun was by far the most beautiful creature he had ever seen, and her love for him was strong. To refuse her offered hand would bring down on him the fierce wrath of a great king, to whom no man said nay.

While Sir Eliduc was in this dilemma, a message came to him from his former master, the Breton king, ordering his immediate return to protect their country from invasion. All Sir Eliduc's love for his own land stirred within him. To defend her borders he was ready to sacrifice his present rank and wealth, and be a simple knight again. The image of his promised wife arose clear and bright before him, and he forgot the lovely Guilliadun, who, for a time, had so dazzled his imagination with her charms.

Laying down his sword before the sovereign, he resigned command of the Exeter troops, and, in spite of the king's rich offers and temptations, hurried to take ship for France. Among his attendants was a youth muffled in a long mantle, who, when they were fairly out at sea, revealed to the knight's astonished gaze the face and form of the wilful Guilliadun.

She had thus disguised herself to follow him, and now vowed that unless he took her to be his wife, she would die by her own fair hand. There was no time for discussion, for, at that moment, arose a mighty tempest which threatened to engulf the ship. In vain were the efforts of the sailors to manage the vessel, and all prepared for immediate death, as wind and waves beat furiously upon them. Suddenly, one of the sailors spoke up for the rest, and, in the hearing of Guilliadun, warned Sir Eliduc that Heaven was angry with him for carrying off the princess in disguise, when he was already promised in marriage to another woman. Guilliadun hearing these words, fell lifeless to the deck. She appeared so like a dead person that the crew offered to throw her overboard, but Eliduc, seizing an oar, struck down the sailor who had spoken, and, himself grasping the helm, drove the ship through foam and boiling waves safely to port. In a few hours he might hope to reach the court of his king; but what, meantime, should he do with the body of the unfortunate princess? In this emergency, he remembered that in a forest near by had once lived an aged hermit, in whose cell he might possibly leave the corpse of the princess, until he should be able to dispose of it in a style suited to her rank. He mounted his palfrey, took the body in his arms, rode to the hermit's retreat, and, gaining entrance to a little chapel, laid on a slab in the centre of it the unhappy Guilliadun.

She was beautiful as ever, and looked like a waxen image. The knight, kneeling beside her, shed many bitter tears, and then, springing to his saddle, galloped off to place himself at the service of his king.

He found the affairs of his country in a bad way, but the mere mention of his name sufficed to inspire the Breton soldiers with new courage. Marching at the head of the king's troops, he led them to battle, and in a short time had put the foe to confusion and rout. Covered with glory, Eliduc rode back to receive the king's congratulations and thanks. There, among the ladies attending the queen, was his faithful Guildeluec; but when she came forward with open arms to greet him, a thought of the Lady Guilliadun, who had died for love of him, shot into his heart like an arrow. Guildeluec quickly saw that something was amiss; but, hiding the anguish she felt, she resolved to keep close watch upon her lover, and, if possible, discover the cause of his coldness.

For some days the court was given up to gaiety and festivals of all kinds. Guildeluec noticed that every day her knight would steal away to the forest and remain there for some hours, returning to the palace more melancholy than before. She set a little page to follow Eliduc, and the boy traced his master to a retreat all overgrown with trees, where the knight entered and was lost to sight.

Dismissing the boy with a piece of gold, the lady resolved herself to unravel the mystery. Wrapped in a long veil, she stole along the green alleys of the wood, and soon reached the little hermitage. Lifting up a curtain of closely woven vines which drooped before it, she entered the chapel door. There, on a bier richly hung with velvet, lay a young and lovely maiden, apparently dead, save that her cheeks bloomed like a new-blown rose. Guildeluec gazed for a while upon this sad sight, when a noise of approaching footsteps startled her, and she hid behind a tomb. The newcomer was none other than the brave knight Eliduc, who, casting himself on the ground beside the bier, gave way to bitter grief, calling the saints above to witness that he had been true to his pledge to Guildeluec, even to hastening to an untimely end the fair maiden before him. Guildeluec heard all, and understood what had taken his love from her. Just then a weasel, running from behind the altar, passed near the bier, which angered the knight, who, at one blow, struck the little animal dead upon the ground. When

Eliduc had gone, the watching lady saw another weasel run up to his slaughtered companion, attempt to play with her, and on finding her without life, go away with every appearance of grief. Directly the weasel came back again, carrying a beautiful red flower from the wood, which was carefully inserted in the mouth of his companion. The effect was magical. Instantly, the dead weasel sprang up, dropped the flower, and scampered off with her happy little comrade.

Guildeluec stooped to pick up the fallen blossom. For a moment she hesitated, for her love for the knight was very great. Then she bent forward, and laid the stem of the flower between the rosy lips of the entranced Guilliadun. Immediately there were signs of life. The girl stirred, a blush came into her cheeks, and her lips parted. When her eyes opened, Guildeluec sighed and said, "Truly, never was there seen so fair a creature."

Guildeluec soon explained to the awakened princess where she was, and received her fervent thanks for delivery from so strange a spell. With many tears, Guilliadun confessed to her unknown friend her love for the knight Eliduc, and the way she had followed him from her father's court. Guildeluec heard her

Guildeluec Reviving Guilliadun.

tale in silence, and when it was at an end, led her away from the hermitage to the palace, where the queen took the princess under her charge, and in the evening presented her with much pomp to the members of her court. When Eliduc saw Guilliadun alive and well, richly clad and lovelier than before, his heart rejoiced, but he turned away from her. Then came forward Guildeluec, who, with the queen's permission, released him from his pledge to her, and gave him back his ring, saying she had determined to retire to a convent and devote her days to holy works.

The queen then placed Guilliadun's hand in that of Eliduc. They were married with great rejoicings; but when the blessing was said over them by the priest, the knight fancied he heard a sigh breathed close in his ear. He looked around; there was no one in sight, save the group of nuns behind a grating, whose voices rose pure and clear in the strains of the bridal hymn.

THE FALCON-KING.

(From one of Marie's Lays.)

THERE lived once, in Britain, an old knight who was lord of Caerwent, a city situated on the River Douglas. He was wealthy and avaricious, and the sole heir to his possessions, a lovely daughter, he kept locked up in a high tower, under the care of a cross governess. His one fear was that this daughter would marry, and thus give some one the right to lay claim to the gold that was dearer to him than life itself. To prevent her from getting a husband, the old knight used every method he could think of to keep off visitors; and any stray caller at the castle was set upon by fierce dogs, who would tear one to pieces as soon as gnaw a beef-bone!

Day after day the father rode off to the hunt, the governess told her beads, and the damsel moped within the tower. One morning she was at her wheel, singing a mournful ditty, and sighing from time to time, as she glanced over the tree-tops at the roofs and spires of the distant city, when suddenly the sky above her window was darkened, and she heard a whirring noise, as of mighty wings astir. A falcon of huge size and noble mien flew in at the casement, and lit submissively at her feet. The maiden stroked his proud head, and at once the bird changed to a beautiful young man, who, in a gentle voice, begged her to have no fear of him, as he was not only a devoted lover but the humblest of her slaves.

"Bid me go if you will," said the prince, "and deeply as I should regret your command, you will see how quickly I shall obey it. Long have I watched you from afar, and dearly I love you. For your sake, I have acquired the art of magic, enabling me to assume this shape in order to reach your prison."

"Oh! but I *don't* want you to go!" cried the poor little mewed-up damsel, who was tired to death of having nobody to talk to.

As she had never seen a man younger than her

father, it was a great astonishment to her to find that the prince's hair was dark and his cheek unwrinkled and rosy as a ripe peach.

What he meant by being a lover, she did not in the least understand. Only, it was pleasant to hear him talk in his kind, low voice; and praises were so rare to her, that they sounded sweet as honey dropping from his lips.

As a matter of course, the afternoon passed quickly; but at last, startled by the noise of a key grating in the lock of the door, the prince quickly assumed his bird-shape, and promising to come again upon the morrow, flew out of the window. The governess could not imagine what had put her prisoner in such a silly state of cheerfulness, as she thought it; and, boxing the poor girl's ears for smiling, gave her a long piece of poetry to learn by heart, and allowed her nothing but bread and water for her tea.

Next day the falcon came again, and for many days he continued his visits, until the girl grew to love him as he loved her, and promised to be his wife. Once a month the chaplain was accustomed to come to see her, and to make her say a catechism the longest ever heard of. When next the day came around for his visit, what was her surprise, instead of the stern chaplain, to find a gentle and kind old priest, who, when left alone with her, avowed himself to be a friend of the falcon-prince.

"As your father is a wicked and unworthy son of the church, and the prince a noble and devoted one, I cannot but approve of the marriage between you and your beloved," the old man said. "The ceremony will now be performed, and may heaven's blessing rest upon you both."

The falcon-prince arrived at the same moment, bearing in his beak a wedding-ring of large bright diamonds. The couple were married, and the prince told his wife that, very soon, he would be able to furnish her also with wings to leave the tower.

One day the governess, coming in unexpectedly, found the girl toying with a beautiful ring, which she hurriedly concealed in her mattress. Spite of all the governess' efforts, she could not find the jewel; nor could she succeed in drawing from her captive any explanation of how she had come by it. The governess told the father, who redoubled his precautions and set spies to watch upon the outside of the tower. In a few days, the spies reported to him that they had seen a bird of the largest size fly in at the maiden's window, remain there for some hours, and then fly out again.

"I'll be a match for this carrier-pigeon of hers!" said the old knight with malicious glee. That night a trap was set upon the outside of the window, surrounded by sharp knives, so that anything passing through it would inevitably be caught or wounded grievously. The young wife awaited her husband anxiously, for it was the day fixed for her escape. Soon he arrived; but as he touched the window the trap fell, and although he managed to pass in, a long trail of blood was left behind him.

"Lose no time, my beloved!" he said, in a voice altered by pain. "Our enemies are upon us. Put this bracelet on your arm, and spring into the air after me, without fear."

She obeyed, and found herself upborne by magic wings, which carried her more swiftly than the wind over forest tops, shining river, and city spires and domes. Glorious as was her airy flight, she could see that her companion grew weaker. They arrived in a country adjoining the one in which she had lived, and stopped immediately above a splendid palace—alighting in the marble balcony of a chamber furnished with the utmost magnificence. Here the falcon regained his man's shape, and, with despair, his wife saw that he was deathly pale, while the blood poured from a wound beneath his heart.

"I am dying," he exclaimed. "Help me to my bed yonder, and may heaven grant me strength to tell my people that you are their lawful queen."

The poor wife aided her husband to lie down, but when he would have spoken to her again, his voice was gone—a moment more, and he was dead.

And now in what a mournful plight the pretty new queen found herself! Soon the attendants would, no doubt, come flocking into the room, to discover their sovereign murdered in his bed, and a stranger cowering by his side. Terror lent speed to her feet, and hastening back to the balcony, she ran down a long flight of stairs communicating with the outer court and garden of the palace. Thence she escaped to wander into the forest, and until day broke again she never ceased to walk. For some days she remained concealed in the forest, living upon fruit and berries, until at last hunger drove her to the cottage of a poor laborer. The wife of this man was very ill, and the queen offered to stay and nurse her, which was gratefully accepted. So faithful and devoted an attendant she proved that, when the woman of the house got well, both husband and wife insisted their stranger guest should make her home with them. In this secluded retreat, where only a stray huntsman now and then passed by, the queen remained until a beautiful son was born to her. And now, she felt a burning desire to have her boy educated in a manner worthy of his father's rank; and poverty, that had seemed so light a burden to herself, grew heavy when it weighed on him. When the baby was three years old, a gay hunting-party passed that way, among them a rich and childless lady, who, charmed with the beauty of the boy, offered to adopt him on the spot.

The poor queen wept so bitterly at thought of parting with her treasure, that the lady, who was a kind-hearted person, proposed she should accompany them and serve in the capacity of the boy's governess.

To this plan the queen made no objection; and, bidding an affectionate farewell to her humble friends, she took her place with the boy in a travelling carriage sent to fetch them.

· · · · · ·

Years rolled on, and the child born in the forest had

reached the age of twenty-one. He was a handsome, manly youth, and skilled in all athletic exercises. About this time, the family of his adopted mother was invited to be present at a great religious ceremony in an abbey upon the borders of a neighboring kingdom. Among the many attendants of the nobles summoned for the occasion, was the real mother, who came dressed in deep mourning and wearing a veil over her face; and one of the guests was the wicked old knight, her father. The abbot of the monastery threw open the doors of the chapel, that had long been sealed, and all flocked into it. There, in the centre, stood a bier covered with cloth of gold and surrounded by blazing wax-lights, while about it knelt an hundred priests, at prayer. After a mass had been sung, the abbot announced that in yonder bier lay the remains of the late king, their master, who, as all his faithful subjects knew, was foully murdered twenty-one years before; and that, by the terms of the king's will, found some time after his death, the throne rightfully belonged to a lady who had been married in secret by their sovereign, and was by him commended to their truest love and honor. "For many long years," added the good abbot, "we have sought vainly for the widow of our lamented ruler; not the faintest trace of her has ever been found, and we have resolved to meet here and choose to-day a successor to our king."

"Here is a worthy successor to your king!" cried a voice from the throng; and the unfortunate queen, throwing back her veil, pointed to her astonished son. "Behold the rightful heir! Who dares to say that he is not the image of his father? *I* am the queen you have so long sought, and this youth is, unknown to himself, my son. In proof of it, here is the marriage ring given me by the king."

"And in proof of it," exclaimed a venerable priest, coming forward, "I attest that *I* performed the marriage ceremony between our king and this poor lady. Her appearance and her claim remove the seal from my promise of secresy, and I unhesitatingly declare this youth to be our lawful sovereign."

All eyes turned upon the young man, and all tongues proclaimed his marvellous resemblance to the king. The abbot knelt at the young man's feet and offered him a golden crown carried on a velvet cushion. Loud cries of joy and cheers filled the air, when suddenly the unfortunate queen was seen to totter toward the bier of her husband.

"I am glad to die on this spot," she said, snatching up the sword that lay upon the tomb and placing it in her son's hand; then, bidding him avenge the sad fate of his parents, she immediately expired. At the same moment, a white-haired knight tried to steal away from the church; but when the ancient priest perceived him, the fugitive was denounced as the murderer of their king. Seized by the populace, the wretched old miser was hurried to instant death; his grandson was carried in triumph to the palace, and there installed as king.

The new monarch reigned long and wisely—an example for all future sovereigns.

EGLAMOUR AND CRYSTABELL.

(From Ellis' Abstract of Copy in Garrick Collection.)

COUNT PRINSAMOUR, an independent sovereign of Artois, was famed for his skill in training young men in the courtesy and accomplishments of chivalry. His court was the resort of all youths who wished to excel in those important arts. His daughter Crystabell, the heiress of Count Prinsamour's dominions, was very beautiful and accomplished, and her father designed to marry her to some powerful monarch. The tournaments instituted at his court were in her honor, and for her sake all the hotheaded young knights in training broke their lances.

Crystabell herself had no desire to leave her own country to become the wife of a foreign monarch. She loved the free and stirring air around her father's castle, and had, unknown to the count, fallen in love with a young knight, Sir Eglamour, who was ever victorious in the numerous tournaments ridden in her name.

Eglamour, on his side, looked up to the young countess as to a star. He never dreamed of winning her love, because he was only a knight, without wealth or lands, depending upon his sword alone to make his way through life. At last, one day, something that Crystabell said made him think that she cared for him more than for the rest of her followers. Sorely troubled, and yet strangely happy, the young man wandered off to think it over. He finally resolved to ask advice of the chamberlain, who had always stood his friend. That personage counselled him to give up all thoughts of the countess, who, he said, was destined by her father to be the bride of a rich and great king. Eglamour sighed, and admitted that his friend was right. But that night, in the solitude of his chamber, he addressed a prayer to God:

> "Lord," he said, "grant me a boon,
>   As thou on rood me bought!
> The erle's daughter, fair and free,
>   That she may my wife be!

> For she is most in my thought:
> That I may wed her to my wife,
> And in joy to lead our life!
> From care then were I brought."

In those days a true knight thought it no shame to his manhood to take the burden of his every-day cares and lay it in all simplicity at the feet of his Maker. When his devotions were at an end, Sir Eglamour slept soundly, and awoke in better heart.

After a while, Sir Eglamour fell ill, and the count desired his daughter, who was skilled in medicine, as were all great ladies of the time, to attend upon the invalid. Crystabell, followed by her damsels, went at once into the sick-room. She found Sir Eglamour feverish and unhappy, and on bending down to minister to him, his pulse throbbed so violently at her touch, that the tears of sympathy came into her eyes. "I have betrayed my love," thought Sir Eglamour; but what was his happiness when the lady bent down to kiss his lips, confessing that the chamberlain had told her what was the real cause of his malady; and, to comfort Eglamour, she bid him live for her sake.

After this, Eglamour got well rapidly; but he felt it right and honorable to inform the count, at once, how matters stood between the two young people. The count, who, although a brave knight, was largely governed by selfish ambition, refused Sir Eglamour with scorn. Then, after thinking a while, he told the youth that he would only bestow his daughter upon the champion who might accomplish three perilous feats of arms, each one of which would expose the candidate to the most imminent danger; and that the victor should not only receive the hand of Crystabell, but in time inherit the whole territory of Artois.

Overjoyed, Sir Eglamour accepted the conditions without delay. He declared he was ready to set off that day or the next upon the enterprise. He did not suspect the count's real purpose in setting him this task, which was to destroy the rash knight who presumed to love his daughter.

"At a little distance to the westward," said the count, "there is a forest of noble trees belonging to a most terrible giant, named Maroke. In a part of the forest shut off for the giant's own hunting ground, are three deer, famed for their size and speed. To hunt one of these celebrated animals is, of course, to challenge an encounter with their owner. Consider whether you have courage enough for such an enterprise."

Sir Eglamour smiled, promised to kill the giant, and hurried off to tell his lady-love. Crystabell trembled and wept, but bid her lover God-speed. She told him that no man ever set forth upon a more arduous journey in a Christian country, but that she gloried in his brave spirit. She gave him a good greyhound, from whom no deer that ever ran had yet escaped—also a sword, once found in the sea, the only one of the kind in the world, and which could carve in two any helmet of steel or iron. Eglamour kissed her farewell, as he received these gifts, and set out with a light heart.

Reaching the giant's park, he followed the wall to a massive gate, burst it open, and entered the wood. This forest was of huge cypress trees, and Eglamour had the luck soon to come upon the three deer grazing quietly. They were the most immense creatures he had ever seen; and singling out the largest, he attacked it. With the help of the dun greyhound, he brought the stag to earth, and set to work to carve his spoil. Laden with venison, he then approached the giant's castle, blowing his horn at intervals; and, when arrived there, he sounded a wild and merry blast, which roused Maroke from sleep and

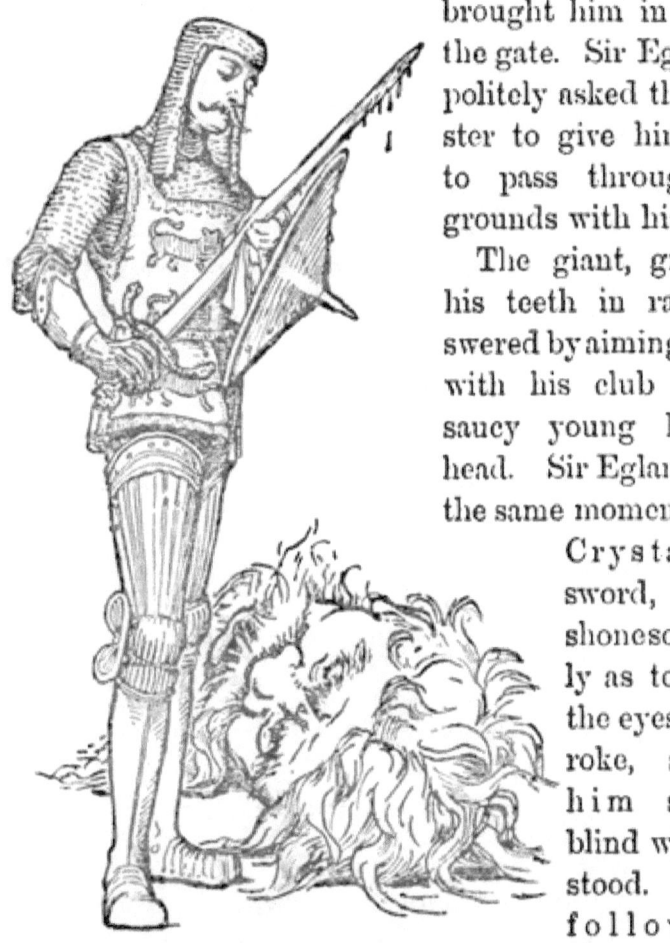

brought him in fury to the gate. Sir Eglamour politely asked the monster to give him leave to pass through the grounds with his prey.

The giant, gnashing his teeth in rage, answered by aiming a blow with his club at the saucy young knight's head. Sir Eglamour, at the same moment, drew Crystabell's sword, which shone so brightly as to dazzle the eyes of Maroke, striking him stone-blind where he stood. Then followed a mighty combat. Blind as the giant was, he fought well and skilfully for three entire days. At the end of the third day, Sir Eglamour rallied all his strength and drove his sword into the giant's heart, a thrust which sent Maroke crashing like a forest tree to earth.

Sir Eglamour, having cut off his enemy's head, carried it, together with the slaughtered stag, back to the court of his sovereign. The count received him ruefully; but fair Crystabell laughed and rejoiced, while the courtiers covered their champion with praises. After Eglamour was rested and refreshed, the count hurried him off again. This time he was to journey to the distant land of Satyn, where his task was to fetch away the head of a prodigious boar, the terror of that ill-fated country, half of whose inhabitants the creature had already eaten up.

To reach the land of Satyn, Sir Eglamour had to travel a fortnight by sea, a fortnight by land. Arriving there at nightfall, he thought it prudent to spend the night in resting on the borders of the forest. At sunrise next day he approached the den of the horrible boar, who had just come back from taking his morning drink in the sea. The animal was a terror to look upon, having flaming eyes and tusks a yard long. He lay gnawing some human bones and growling frightfully, surrounded by dead bodies, many of which were clad in knightly armor. At once Sir Eglamour dashed at him with a shout—" For God and Crystabell ! " The boar whetted his long tusks and set upon his adversary, killing at the first blow Sir Eglamour's noble horse, his own tough hide remaining unhurt by the spear. Sir Eglamour now had recourse to his magic sword, and found to his joy that, wherever he struck, the boar's hide was cut; although the length of the animal's tusks made it difficult to close with him. This combat, like that with the giant, lasted three days, and at the end Sir Eglamour, by a sudden swift movement, made a terrible blow at the creature's neck, severing the head from his body.

Long before the close of this memorable fight, the boar's snorts of rage and defiance had attracted to the spot the King of Satyn and fifteen of his knights, who happened to be hunting in the forest. When the boar dropped dead, Sir Eglamour fell over him, and lay there completely exhausted. The king and his men drew near, showered compliments on the strange knight's bravery, and told him that the wicked beast of whom he had rid them had sometimes destroyed as many as forty men in one day.

The king ordered a cloth to be laid upon the grass, and Sir Eglamour was regaled with venison and rich wine, which brought strength back to his arm and hope to his heart. The king's men then attempted to cut up the boar, but failed, owing to the toughness of his hide. The sword of Sir Eglamour was put into requisition, and in a moment the beast was cleft asunder along the back bone. The meat was distributed among the knights and men-at-arms, Sir Eglamour claiming the head alone. The King of Satyn afterward ordered for the champion a warm bath of certain sweet-scented herbs that healed his wounds and in which he rested pleasantly till break of day. Then the party went on to the king's palace, where Sir Eglamour was asked to stay and recover from his fatigue.

Now it happened that the boar just slain was an intimate friend of Manas, a huge and frightful giant, own brother to Maroke. Manas had fallen in love with the King of Satyn's daughter, and had vowed to carry her off. When Manas came prowling around the castle that evening, and beheld on the point of a spear over the gateway the head of his friend the boar, he flew into an awful passion, foaming at the mouth; and as he looked on that head—

"Alas!" he cried, "art thou dead?
  My trust was all in thee!
Now, by the law that I live in,
My little speckled hoglin,
  Dear bought shall thy death be!"

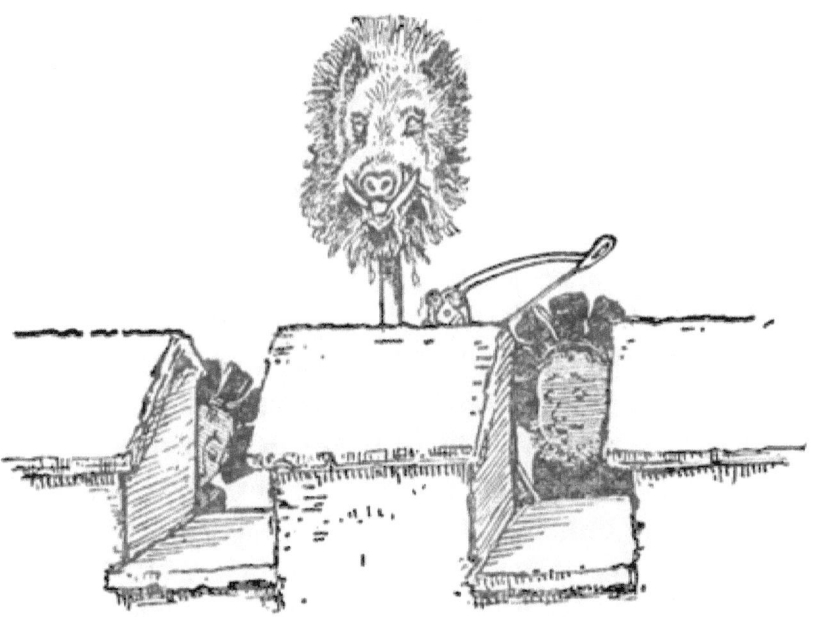

Manas beat upon the door and walls of the castle in a fury, demanding the surrender of the murderer of his dear little speckled hoglin. Presently, Sir Eglamour, fully armed and equipped, mounted on a fiery courser, and with lance in rest, attacked the giant at full speed.

Manas resisted vigorously, and in an instant overthrew man and horse. The king, the princess, and the court, who had assembled on the walls of the castle, began to tremble for the safety of their champion. But Sir Eglamour, lightly springing to his feet, drew his invincible sword, and closing with the giant, cut off his right arm. The monster roared with pain, but continued to fight, though yelling at intervals as loudly as ever, till near sunset, when the patient knight, who had hitherto suffered him to exhaust himself by his own efforts, suddenly rushed forward and completed the victory! The boar and Manas being dead, Eglamour now took his leave of the grateful King of Satyn and his court, who rejoiced greatly over the death of their two adversaries. The heads of the boar and the giant Manas were carefully packed up, and in due time Eglamour laid them at the feet of his faithful Crystabell.

Count Prinsamour, secretly disgusted at his knight's success, at once sent him off on another enterprise, more dangerous than the two preceding ones. Eglamour and Crystabell, now seeing that the false count was determined to prevent their marriage, parted from each other with many tears. But Crystabell vowed to marry him, with or without her father's leave, so soon as he should return, if ever he did, from the present journey.

The third mission was to kill a tremendous dragon, at that time desolating the country around the gates of Rome. After sundry adventures by the way, Eglamour encountered the beast, and fought it long and valiantly. He succeeded in cutting off its wings, tail, and head; but at last he fell himself, exhausted by his wounds and poisoned by the dragon's sting, and was carried from the field.

When Crystabell heard that her brave lover was lying at the point of death in Rome, she left her father and journeyed to the knight's bedside, where, to make him happy before he died, she consented to marry him on the spot.

Eglamour rallied under the care of his beloved Crystabell; but, after they had spent some happy months together, Count Prinsamour found out his daughter's place of retreat, and carried her off from her husband, abusing him as a vile thief and imposter.

Crystabell cried and lamented continually for her lost husband. After a while, a son was born to her, which made the count more angry than before. He took the unfortunate mother and child, put them, without food, into an open boat, and set them adrift upon the sea. The boat drifted for five days, and at last reached the shores of a country whose king proved to be the brother of Crystabell's own mother. He took the wayfarers under his care, and devoted himself to bringing up the boy, named Degrabell, to be a valiant knight.

After a time, Eglamour travelled to Artois, and entering the count's hall by force, confronted his cruel father-in-law in the presence of all the knights and squires. He had heard of the fate of his wife and child, and his wrath was terrible to see. He cast the dragon's head, wings, and tail before the count, reminded him that his daughter had been fairly won, and called down God's judgment upon the unnatural father who had bereaved Eglamour of all he held dear in life. The count retreated to his strongest citadel in fear before the righteous anger of this mighty champion; but Eglamour seized the property of his late master, divided it among the count's worthy and needy subjects, and ordering masses to be sung in all the churches for the soul of his lost Crystabell, departed for the Holy Land, where, during many years, he distinguished himself both in battle and in tournament against the Saracens.

When her son, Sir Degrabell, had reached the age of eighteen, Crystabell was more beautiful than ever, and the king, her uncle, resolved to marry her to some knight who might make happy the remainder of her days. Crystabell, who still cherished the memory of her lost Sir Eglamour, begged her son to help her in this emergency. Sir Degrabell went to the king and insisted that all of the knights aspiring to his mother's hand should first meet him in the lists, and that only the one who should overthrow him might claim the princess as a wife.

The king smiled at the pretentions of this beardless youth, and gave his consent. A tournament was announced, and to it came from all parts of the country persons of high rank seeking adventure. Knight after knight presented himself in the lists, and was swiftly unhorsed by the gallant Degrabell. At length the boy, flushed with conquest, turned to a stranger of distinguished appearance who stood gazing at the spectacle, without seeming to take any great interest in it, and asked if he too had a mind to break a lance.

The stranger knight hesitated, then said that, to amuse himself, he would do so. Mounting his horse, he rode with the speed of a lightning flash against Degrabell, who was borne to the earth on the spot. Princess Crystabell had been watching the tourney with pride, but screamed aloud at her son's overthrow, and rushed into the arena, throwing herself on her knees before the stranger and imploring him to spare her boy. Trembling, she looked upon the victor's shield, and there saw depicted a rude device of a golden boat containing a lady and a child about to perish in the waves.

On his side, the knight gazed at the lady in trembling, then bending his knee before her, revealed himself the long-lost Eglamour. Crystabell would have swooned for joy, had not her husband caught her in his arms. Eglamour, equally astonished and delighted, had still in store for him the rapture of recognizing in his brave young antagonist the son so worthy of his sire.

Sir Eglamour and Lady Crystabell, thus happily reunited, lived together for the remainder of their days in prosperity. Degrabell became a famous champion. The old Count Prinsamour broke his neck by falling from his tower; and so, my tale is told!

www.ingramcontent.com/pod-product-compliance
Lightning Source LLC
Chambersburg PA
CBHW020320240426
43673CB00039B/866